THE PRISONER
AND THE BOMB

Laurens van der Post

THE PRISONER AND THE BOMB

British Title: The Night of the New Moon

WILLIAM MORROW AND COMPANY, INC., 1971

New York

Published in the United States in 1971.

Copyright © 1970 by Laurens van der Post

Published in Great Britain in 1970.

Printed in the United States of America by
The Maple Press Company, York, Pennsylvania.

Library of Congress Catalog Card Number 79-134487

FOR "NICK"
the Wing-Commander W. T. H. Nichols
of this story, because without him
and his steadfastness there might have
been neither story-teller nor story to tell.

CONTENTS

PROLOGUE

I WOULD NOT HAVE thought it possible I could ever have forgotten that an anniversary of the utmost significance for me fell on August 6th. Indeed, so profound a part of my memory had it become that hitherto, without any conscious help from me, my eyes had only to see the dateline on my morning newspaper and the memory of what it all had meant in my own life and the life of our time would erupt like a volcano in my imagination. And yet, there it was: I *had* forgotten the date until the moment I walked into that television studio in America at about six o'clock in the evening of Wednesday, August 6th.

I was due to be interviewed about Africa in some current affairs program. All day long my mind had been trying to concern itself with my native continent. It is a concern which normally comes to me easily. Yet, on this occasion I had been aware of some unusual resistance in my mind to directing itself to the problems of Africa, no matter how urgent they appeared on the surface. The meaning of this resistance only became clear when I arrived in the studio and saw the man who was already in the process of being interviewed on the same program for the ten minutes before I myself had to appear. He was Japanese, a man I guessed to be about seventy years of age, with close-cropped grey hair. He was small even for a Japanese who had been born in the time of the great Emperor Meiji, when the Japanese on the average were smaller than they are today, and his smallness somehow was emphasized not only by the contrast with the tall, robust young American who was interviewing him, but also by his desperate struggle to speak English on a subject so obviously charged with emotion for him. The smallness struck me as singularly poignant, almost as if it were universally symbolic and personified how small and in need of help we all are in the face of the great reckonings life keeps on forcing on us, like the one of which he was trying to speak. He and his interviewer sat there on a raised platform in front of me—the most powerful lights of the studio focussed on them. By contrast the greater part of the studio was in darkness, silent except for the sibilant and limping English of this shrivelled little Japanese gentleman, and, as the sight of him brought this volcano of which I have spoken to the boil in my imagination, I felt almost as if I were looking not at a scene contrived in the physical here and now so much as something lit by some strange ectoplasmic glow in the innermost chamber of my own mind. I do not know which was the greater then: the violence of the eruption that followed or the feeling of personal dismay which accompanied it, since if *I* could forget, how could anybody else ever be expected to remember the day as I had known it? It was, of course, the anniversary of the dropping of the first atom bomb on Hiroshima, and the young American interviewer was extracting, with skill and delicacy, from the little old Japanese gentleman his experience of that great and terrible day.

He was, he said, a doctor. Both he and his wife were Christians. He was at work in his surgery and his wife was in the Japanese equivalent of a drawing-room, sitting at her harmonium. He could hear her playing a Christian hymn—no, he no longer remembered which particular hymn it was because his mind was on medical things and he heard it only in snatches. In any case, the shock of the horror that followed had been so great that to this day he found it difficult if not impossible to remember what had happened immediately before. Besides she had not been at the harmonium long when the bomb fell. She and his four children in other parts of their house were killed instantly; he, miraculously, was spared.

He said this with a nervous sort of smile, which I doubt if anybody else who noticed it understood, but which moved me almost to tears, because it was the kind of smile which comes almost by reflex to the Japanese, who attach so much importance to good manners, in order that it should lighten for others the impact of the news of any personal tragedy which they may have had to impart. My long experience of this remarkable people had taught me that, the greater the tragedy, the greater the compulsion to make light of it before the world. I stood there then for some seven more minutes while he was made to tell in great detail his experience, from the moment the bomb fell to what he finally saw when he crawled out of the ruins of his own house to look for help in the shattered city outside. The detail needs no repetition here because it has all been minutely recorded, is well known, and is the one part of the story told over and over again, to such an extent that it presents itself on the scene of the contemporary mind as it would have been presented on millions of television screens in America that evening as the full story of that great and terrible day.

As I stood there caught between the turmoil of my own associations with the day and the horror of Hiroshima, it suddenly seemed to me to be important that both Hiroshima and Nagasaki, which followed, were only part of a greater whole and that this whole, as far as I knew, had never been adequately reported. I began to feel that I must hasten to do so before it was too late. The imagination of our time, particularly the imagination of the young who have been born since Hiroshima, know only this part of the story. As a result, we accept, like this young American interviewer—he could have been no more than five at the time of Hiroshima—that this tragic Japanese version is an authentic microcosm of the macrocosm of the whole truth. This aspect suddenly seemed of such overwhelming importance to me that I was compelled to immediate action.

All this while, the producer of the program, who had brought me into the studio, had been standing silent at my side, caught up in the horror of the story as had been everyone else, from cameramen and their assistants to interviewer. I took him by the arm and drew him with me out of the studio. He followed like someone coming out of a trance. I closed the door silently behind us and begged him to forget all about Africa. I told him that I too had been involved in the tragedy of Hiroshima. No, I had not been in Hiroshima itself. I had been thousands of miles away in Java, but what had happened to me in Java was as much part of the story of Hiroshima and Nagasaki as what had happened to the people in the doomed cities themselves. Like all planners, he had a mystique about planning and hated any change of direction. But we had worked together before, and in the end my argument that it would be wrong to let only this one Japanese voice, authentic as it was, speak for the day, won him over. He agreed to allow me, at the end of the prescribed moment, to take over from his interviewer and to put to the little Japanese doctor my own version of the day.

So it happened that when the official interviewer ended, the voice of the producer announced a change of plan, saying that instead of speaking on Africa I, who had been a Japanese prisoner-of-war for three and a half years, would have a discussion about Hiroshima with the Japanese doctor. I had only ten minutes for a long and complex story but I remember beginning by trying to reassure the Japanese doctor, more tense than ever at this unexpected elaboration of his interview, that I wanted to tell him something which I hoped would help him to make his peace with the tragedy of Hiroshima even more effectively than with his obvious magnanimity he had already done. If I remember rightly I began saying all this very badly in Japanese, not only to reassure him but as the only means available to me of showing him how involved I felt with him and his people in what had happened on that day. I went on then as quickly as I could, in English, to tell him my part of that story. What follows is an orchestration of what I told him, but it reflects much more accurately the spirit of our brief confrontation, in that strange subliminal light of a transitory television set-up, that it is in a living sense far more truthful than a literal transcript of the occasion could be. Truth after all is always so much more than fact.

STORY

The depth of darkness into which you can descend, and still live, is an exact measure, I believe, of the height to which you can aspire to reach.

LETTER FROM ALAN MACGLASHAN TO THE WRITER

I BEGAN BY TRYING to describe to the Japanese doctor what life had been like in a Japanese prisoner-of-war camp, because he confessed that even after all this time he personally had taken no interest in the matter and had read no literature about it. I tried to make my description as factual as possible and to keep my own personal emotions out of it, which was not as difficult as it may sound because I had for many years now looked repeatedly and deeply into the experience and it had, I truly believe, left nothing bitter or destructive in my mind. I barely mentioned the physical brutalities we had experienced at the hands of our Japanese guards and particularly at the hands of their Korean converts who increasingly took over from them as the war effort demanded more and more of the Japanese. But they, in the manner of all converts, became much more fanatical than their converters until they were caricatures of the worst kind of Japanese. I skimmed over the grimmest of my own experiences. For instance, I said little of how before I was brought into a so-called Japanese regular prisoner-of-war camp I had been made to watch Japanese soldiers having bayonet practice on live prisoners-of-war tied between bamboo posts; had been taken to witness executions of persons of all races and nationalities, for obscure reasons like "showing a spirit of wilfulness," or not bowing with sufficient alacrity in the direction of the rising sun.

I could have digressed on this one fact of my experiences for hours, because I would never have thought it possible that in our time there could still have been so many different ways of killing people—from cutting off their heads with swords, bayonetting them in the many variations of the ways I have mentioned, to strangling them and burying them alive; but most significantly, never by just shooting them.

I say "significantly" because the omission of this contemporary form of killing was for me the most striking evidence of the remote and archaic nature of the forces which had invaded the Japanese spirit, blocking out completely the light of the twentieth-century day. It was, indeed, the awareness of this dark invasion which made it impossible for people like ourselves, even at our worst moments in prison, to have any personal feelings against our captors, because it made us realize how the Japanese were themselves the puppets of immense impersonal forces to such an extent that they truly did not know what they were doing.

It was amazing how often and how many of my men would confess to me, after some Japanese excess worse than usual, that for the first time in their lives they had realized the truth, and the dynamic liberating power of the first of the Crucifixion utterances: "Forgive them for they know not what they do."

I found the moment they grasped this fundamental

fact of our prison situation, forgiveness became a product not of an act of will or of personal virtue even, but an automatic and all-compelling consequence of a law of understanding: as real and indestructible as Newton's law of gravity. The tables of the spirit would be strangely and promptly turned and we would find ourselves without self-pity of any kind, feeling deeply sorry for the Japanese as if we were the free men and they the prisoners—men held in some profound *oubliette* of their own minds.

Accordingly, this aspect of our imprisonment at that moment in the studio seemed so unimportant if not altogether irrelevant that it was easily and quickly disposed of. What needed stressing more was that by the beginning of 1945 we were all physically dying men. For more than three years the Japanese had steadily cut down our rations. In other parts of Southeast Asia, in Malaya, in Burma and on the notorious Siamese railroad, there might have been some excuse that food for their prisoners had to be imported and that as the tide of war turned inexorably against them their means of importing food failed them and they could not, had they wished to do so, have increased the rations for their prisoners. I myself cannot speak with any degree of personal certainty about that, because the whole of that field of war lay outside my own experience. All I could say was that in Java, where we were, there was no such excuse, because throughout the three and a half years of the Japanese occupation of Indonesia there was no scarcity of food in the land.

The Dutch had made Java one of the most highly organized and richest rice-producing countries in the world. On the Bandoeng plateau alone, where I endured most of my captivity, the agricultural economy had been raised to such a pitch of efficiency that the Javanese farmers, in a climate that was for ever one long afternoon of summer, harvested rice five times in every two years. There was always a surplus of rice at least, not to speak of surpluses of protein substances like the *kachang-idjoe,* a Javanese form of the pea and a valuable leguminous cereal, or the eggs of the ducks bred in millions in the water-filled paddies of that singularly blessed and rich volcanic island. Yet it had been the Japanese policy consistently to reduce our rations to such an extent that the daily portion of rice, which was almost our only food, fell in three years from five hundred grams per man a day to ninety grams—a fraction over three ounces. There was not a person in my own prisoner-of-war camp in 1945 who was not suffering from deficiency diseases of some kind; beri-beri and pellagra were, as far as we were concerned, the least of them. The ones most feared were the many complex and painful kinds of malnutritional neuritis, which made men's nerves burn so much with pain that they could not sleep at night, and in many cases deprived them of their sight or lowered their moral and physical resistance so much that they died of afflictions which in normal conditions would not have compelled them to take to their beds.

Indeed the mortality rate among us, I am certain,

would have been close to the mortality rate of a German concentration camp if it had not been for the Chinese in Java. These remarkable people, just on my verbal promise that I, whose chances of survival were of the slimmest, would see that the British Government repaid them at the end of the war, smuggled thousands of guilders for me into the camp. With these guilders we were able to supplement our diet by buying fresh fruit and cereals through the Japanese and Koreans who of course had their own financial interest in these transactions.

However, these supplementary sources of food dwindled steadily throughout 1945, not only because the Japanese attitude to us hardened rapidly in proportion to the accelerating degree in which the war was turning against them, but also because of inflation. The Javanese guilder, which at the beginning of my own term of imprisonment had enabled me, for instance, to buy ducks' eggs at one and a half cents each, had so declined in value by August 1945 that we were paying as much as ten *guilders* for the same egg—on paper an increase in price of over sixty thousand per cent! Such eggs and cereals as we could buy had to be used literally only for people in danger of dying—and by August almost all of us were on the fringe of this. Some drawings I possess of scenes in prison, done even some months before the beginning of this grimmest of all months, reveal to me today faces and bodies of men already not altogether unlike those of the inmates of Belsen.

I remember vividly how the senior British officer and I reviewed our situation with the band of remarkable Dutch and British doctors who were in prison with us. The senior British officer was a wing-commander in the Royal Air Force, a man called Nichols. Some day I hope to write more about Nichols and all that the thousands of men who were in prison with him owe him. He was one of the most extraordinary-ordinary individuals I have ever met. He had, in a way which was quint-essentially English, both immense physical and moral courage of the most unobtrusive kind: always there to be called upon when needed, almost as if they were part of the routine of his quiet spirit, to be exercised in moments of crisis, however potentially disastrous, with a sort of understatement of behaviour which never failed to have the effect of lowering the mounting fever of rage in our captors. Moreover, courage was so natu-ral to him that in all the long inarticulate years in prison I never once detected any indication that the abnormal stresses of our captivity affected his capacity for com-mand, as they sometimes did in officers with far less res-ponsibility.

Unfortunately, this is not the place for the portrait which is needed of this remarkable man. All I need stress is that when, some months after the surrender in Java, I joined him already in prison, we had agreed that if we were to live as prisoners in a creative and dignified way, let alone survive, one of the first things we had to do was never to take refuge in comfortable illusions but always try to look the truth, however grim, straight in the eye. One of the most important aspects of this, it seemed to us, was to make as accurate as possible an assessment of how long our imprisonment was likely to last, and to face our men openly with our conclusions. This seemed to me not only fundamental but urgent because, at the time, another school of thought ruled the minds of thousands of men in prison with us.

Most of the prisoners were Dutch and hundreds of the remnants of their Christian Ambonese and Menadonese battalions and sprinklings of Chinese, suspected of being sympathetic to the Allied cause. The Dutch officers had decided that the only way of getting their men to make the best of their imprisonment was to live on the assumption that their liberation was near.

As a result they filled the camps with fresh rumours each day of fantastic Allied victories, mostly of impossible American landings on neighboring islands and impending invasions of Java and Sumatra. The fantasy and ingenuity that went into the invention of unreal rumours of this kind had to be experienced to be believed.

There was one school of thought, for instance, which carried this process so far that it asserted, a year before the end, that the Japanese were already defeated and for reasons of high Allied strategy were merely holding us technically in prison until the onerous logistics of taking over the administration of the island and evacuating us all could be organized.

This was mad, of course, and touching evidence of how shattered the colonial Dutch had been by their

defeat and how profound the fears aroused in their
unconscious by their plight under the unpredictable,
impervious and, for the moment, all-powerful Japanese
army.

Both Nichols and I thought that only moral disinte-
gration and disaster could lie in such a method of command. So as far back as August 1942, we had come to
the conclusion that with Rommel almost at Alexandria,
Hitler in the suburbs of Moscow and Leningrad, the
Japanese pushing on towards Port Moresby in New
Guinea and apparently on the verge of invading Australia itself, with the whole of the Dutch East Indies,
the third largest empire in the world, in their possession, Malaya and Burma fallen and their armies batter-
ing against a thin British-Indian-army line on the
borders of India itself; with large parts of the Pacific
Ocean as well as the seas of Southeast Asia and the
Bay of Bengal in their power, we could easily be in
prison for anything from five to twelve years. We told
our men the worst and prepared them for a life of
twelve years in prison.

What we did not tell them was that Nichols and I
differed as to whether we had a reasonable chance
of coming through imprisonment alive. He himself
doubted it, and with his respect for the truth thought
he ought to tell—if not our men—then at least our
officers. I disagreed with him, not because I was afraid
that our officers and men were incapable of enduring
the worst, but because at the time I myself had no inner
conviction or even glimmer of intuition as to what our

ultimate fate would be. I felt that there was an enormous difference between conveying one's fears, as opposed to one's convictions, to the people under our command.

I had many fears myself and knew that Nichols' own could easily prove right. But until fear proved a certainty I felt strongly that we had to contain it within ourselves. Our only answer, it seemed to me, was to live our days in prison as if we were men committed to live to the end of our natural term on earth.

In return I promised Nichols that I myself would make it my special duty to keep constantly under review the possibility that we might not come out of prison alive. In so far as this possibility existed, it had two profound roots in reality; the first and most obvious one being that we might not survive because of lack of food and the inability of our undernourished bodies to withstand the onslaught of any of the infections endemic in the East. The other was rooted in the character of the Japanese military: their contempt for prisoners-of-war, all the greater because they themselves regarded captivity as the final degradation of the male spirit, and would and indeed did take their own lives in hundreds of thousands rather than endure the disgrace of falling into enemy hands. This contempt was reinforced by the profound disregard of the importance of life on earth implicit in their culture, and their belief that the life of an individual man was of "no more account than a feather."

More dangerous still was the fact that, consciously or

unconsciously, they were instruments of complicated processes of a kind of accumulated revenge of history on the European for his invasion of the ancient worlds of the East and his arrogant assumptions of superiority which had made him use his power in the physical world to bend the lives and spirits of the people of Asia to his inflexible will. The fact that the European had brought also to the Far East his great Roman virtues was for the moment forgotten. All that mattered was that for centuries his powerful presence had prevented the peoples of the Far East, so diverse in character and culture, from being their own special selves.

These processes of frustration indeed had been carried on for so long that it was almost as if the peoples of Asia had only come into the presence of a European to be hypnotized out of being themselves, and forced to live a kind of tranced life in his presence that was not their own. But now the spell was broken, and the built-up flood of resentment following centuries of frustration had broken through all restraints. Out in full spate, in the open at last, it swept the Japanese, normally so disciplined, but now drunk on what for the moment appeared to be invincible military power, into a chaotic mood of revenge on those who belonged to the world which had been responsible for that resentment.

Again, I could write a book on this aspect of our imprisonment alone, because I had already been aware of it on my first visit to Japan, as far back as 1926, and had come away from the Far East knowing that these forces, of the "vengeance of history" as I called it to myself even then, had already been set in motion by the Japanese victory in their war against the Russians at the beginning of the century, and were steadily gathering strength beneath the rough surface of the international scene.

So much were the Japanese themselves caught up in the psychology of this aspect of their conquest that it completely dominated their view of their European prisoners. They never saw us as human beings, but as provocative symbols of a detested past. They had only to look at us for this urge of resentment to quicken in their blood to such an extent that I still marvel not so much at the excesses they perpetrated as at their restraint.

I remember saying to Nichols at the time that one of our gravest dangers was that we were imprisoned at a moment when not just the chickens but all the *pterodactyls* of our history in the Far East had come home to roost. Throughout our imprisonment this was, I believe, one of the elements most threatening to our survival and the genuine cause of the gravest excesses that were inflicted on us from time to time.

I myself had no doubt that in time the Japanese would be defeated, but what I could not tell, in the light of all this, was how they could ever be defeated in such a manner that they themselves would be relieved of these overwhelming compulsions, of this unconscious sense of a duty, a mission, of history, to

carry the feud aflame in their blood to a final cataclysmic end in which they and all the people they had
captured would have to perish.

I knew of no nation at the time for whom honour,
however perverted, was so great a necessity as for the
Japanese. Honour, and a life in which they did not lose
honour with themselves seemed to them as important
as, if not more important than, food. I knew their history and their literature well. I needed no reminders,
even in prison, of the destructive forms their individual
and collective sense of honour could assume.

I was convinced of only one thing: that unless they
could be defeated in such a way that they were not deprived of their honour by defeat, there was nothing but
disaster for them and us in the end. This, more even
than starvation or disease, I saw as the real danger that
would threaten us every minute of the days and nights
of our long years of captivity, either through a breakdown in the restraint of an individual Japanese commander and his guards, or through the deliberate
choice of the overall Japanese command to pull down
their own sprawling military temple, Samson-like, and
to destroy the European Philistine along with themselves rather than endure defeat with ignominy.

I found proof of all this in the fact that as the war
turned increasingly against them our own treatment
became harsher. Almost everyone in prison with me
reasoned all the time that as the Japanese increasingly
saw ultimate defeat approaching they would become
more lenient in their treatment of their captives be-

cause of a mounting desire to appease the victors on the day of surrender. I took the opposite view and my sense of our peril in this regard rapidly heightened as the year 1945 advanced, and became singularly acute from the moment of the German surrender.

By this time this sense of peril did not depend as it had done in the beginning solely on my reading of history and my understanding of the Japanese national character, but also on concrete intelligence. Apart from ensuring our survival by smuggling money for the purchase of food into our camp from the Chinese whom I have mentioned, which I had in agreement with Nichols made one of my special duties, I had also taken upon myself freely the task of accumulating all the intelligence I could about life outside our prison walls; particularly of the nature and extent of the forces of nationalism stirring in the islands, as well as the conscious policy and plans, of the Japanese military.

Intelligence in the first category was comparatively easy to organize. Through my Chinese friends again a steady flow of information reached me in camp, and never once dried up until near the end. Through them I knew in minute and accurate detail of the new mood and temper of the indigenous peoples outside, and this was to prove of extreme value to our High Command after the Japanese capitulation. For the Allies arrived in that secluded theater of war without intelligence of any kind in the real sense of the term.

But more relevant to the immediate theme, I knew about all the prisons for soldiers, European civilians and Eurasians that the Japanese had established all over the islands.

I knew that in Java alone close on 100,000 Europeans were impounded in Japanese prisons, in very much the same conditions as those in which we were being held, and that for them too the conditions of imprisonment were daily deteriorating in an alarming fashion. I was able to form some idea of the total numbers of people the Japanese had imprisoned in the outer islands of Indonesia, as well as in Malaya, Thailand, the old French Indo-China and Borneo; and though I could not put an accurate number to the total it was clear that it ran into hundreds of thousands.

Far more difficult was the problem of intelligence about Japanese military policy. I had only two sources from which I could gather this. One was from a secret radio which a small group of officers operated under my direction.

Both Nichols and I, in spite of the fact that if the radio were discovered not only the officers but we ourselves would be promptly executed, as some officers and men had already been for the same reason in another camp, thought it imperative to run the risk. We regarded accurate knowledge of how the war was going as of fundamental importance in our battle for the truth, which was the foundation of all we did for our men in the camp and which determined the use we made of our slender resources for supplementing our inadequate and shrinking diet.

It was our only sure defense against slow demoralization by the fantasies and illusions which the infinitely resourceful and wishful rumourmongering of a world in isolation and constant peril was perpetually pitting against the sense of reality of the thousands of men and officers under our command. So, despite the obvious risks, we operated a secret radio throughout our period of imprisonment.

How the radio was built and run by a few resourceful and gallant young officers, their many hair-raising escapes from detection, is again a story in itself. However, all that is relevant here is that without the intelligence provided by this radio we could not have lived our life in prison in what I believe was the triumphant manner we did.

Through this radio, too, I always had an exact picture of how the war against Japan was going, and this picture unfortunately heightened my sense of the special peril of which I have spoken; because nowhere in any of the many theaters of the campaign in Asia did it show, either in the minds of those responsible for Allied war policy or those of the enemy, the slightest hint of what the Japanese would regard as an "honourable" alternative to fighting according to the logic of their spirit, and their sense of history: namely the annihilation of themselves and of all those of their enemies whom they held as prisoners.

Then, suddenly, towards the end of 1944, by what seemed to me at the time a miracle, I established contact with a source which enabled me to look as it were through a keyhole into the minds and intentions of the

Japanese military command. I owed this again to my Chinese friends still at liberty outside our prison walls.

They sent me a message one day that a Korean Christian working for the Japanese military intelligence in the island had asked to be put in touch with me.

At first I feared a trap, and for many weeks I sent no reply to his offer. For once I did not even consult Nichols, who was so close to me, because I felt it vital that, if I accepted the offer and it proved a trap, he should in no way be involved and that I alone should pay the penalty, which would, of course, have been death by one of the several disagreeable forms of execution I had witnessed.

I do not know, however, whether I would have taken up the contact, much as it might have helped me, if despite my silence, this Korean had not begun to send me scraps of information which were proved true by subsequent events and were of real value to us.

He would inform me, for instance, that the Japanese were planning to send some hundreds of prisoners from other parts of the island to join us. He would give me both numbers and dates accurately, and well in advance, so that we could make plans for their reception and readjust our resources accordingly. He it was, for example, who told me of the coming of a party of British prisoners-of-war who had been sent not long after our capitulation to build an aerodrome on the small island of Haruko, near the greater island of Ambon in the far east of the Javanese Archipelago. He told me how hundreds of them had died on the island, through both the inefficiency of the Japanese system of logistics and the brutality of the Japanese military in command there. He said that the prisoners were coming back starved and dying, travelling in such terrible conditions that not many of them would survive the journey. He also warned me that the members of the Japanese prison staff responsible for the worst of the atrocities on Haruko would be returning with the party, to assume positions of high responsibility in prisoner-of-war camps in Java.

This communication from him, even in the staccato form of transmission in which it reached me through the Chinese, proved not only to be true, but established clearly that, to know details of events so far away from Java and of plans so far in advance, he must occupy a central position in the Japanese system of intelligence.

I think none of us who saw the day his story proved true could possibly ever forget it, because the few survivors of an original party of some fifteen hundred men who came into camp looked like pictures of the last inmates of Belsen on the day of their liberation. The story of their journey from Haruko to Java was in every way as terrible as my Korean informant had predicted.

Among the survivors was a Royal Air Force officer whom I had known well. Yet I did not recognize him until he spoke his name, "Blackwood." He did so in a voice which I could hardly hear. Blackwood told me that on the long journey by sea, in a small ship short of water and food, guarded by soldiers who never went short of either, his men died so fast that they were throwing the corpses over the side at the rate of seventeen to twenty-seven a day and that they hardly had the strength to do even that.

Moreover the worst of their guards appeared on the staff of our own camp, like the unbelievable warrant officer Gunzo Mori and his Korean satellite—a tiny young man of unlimited energies, resource, and variety of mood: a complex mixture of extreme sadistic impulses and unpredictable generosity, who had adopted the Japanese name of Kasayama and who was to be condemned later by a war crimes tribunal to death by hanging, side by side with his Japanese overlord.

Their end has never ceased to haunt me, because in the thick fog of unknowing that enshrouded the spirit of our captors these two, Mori and Kasayama, among all the many extremes of character I met, seemed to me to know the least what they were doing.

Yet even this, important as it is to me, is not the reason why I mention the Haruko incident. I do so because of the role it played in making me begin to realize how reliable and valuable an informant the Korean on the Japanese staff could be. By way of confirmation, soon after this he told me of a plan to move hundreds of the fittest of our men and officers to work on some Japanese scheme in Sumatra.

Without yet committing myself fully to a system of exchange with him, beyond a brief word of thanks delivered through the Chinese, I took him at his word and warned Nichols, so that it enabled us to select the fittest among our men and officers for this move, and to put them on as generous a diet as we could afford, so that they would have the greatest possible chance of surviving the ordeal in front of them.

With the impact of Haruko still fresh in our minds, we had no doubt that the ordeal would be extreme and that even with a maximum increase in their diet, considering at what a low level the physical stamina of the average person in camp already was, few of them might survive the experience.

This forewarning alone put us in debt to this Korean, for without it I am certain most of this great working party, which indeed left our camp for Sumatra some weeks later, could not have survived—as we were overjoyed to find at the end of the war they had mostly done.

From this moment on I was convinced that I had no option but to do all I could to encourage this contact. Yet I was still not sure that all this might not be some bait, some subtle Japanese means of finding out whether I, who had been released in the beginning into a regular prisoner-of-war camp under extreme suspicion, and had been lucky indeed to escape instant execution after my capture, was not plotting in some way against them—though heaven knows what one could possibly have plotted in such horribly reduced and restricted circumstances!

I am ashamed to say that this suspicion of my Korean informant never entirely left me until the end, and that

I took the utmost precautions in any answers I sent him
to make them as innocent as possible; though I knew
that if the Japanese ever discovered that I had been in
touch with him at all, no innocence of answer on my
part would be enough to save me from extreme retribution. I doubt whether I would have been able to
persuade myself to continue some eighteen months of
underground association with him in spite of the use-
fulness of his information if it had not been for three
factors: one, that my Chinese friends obviously trusted
him and that they themselves were never exposed and
never got into trouble with the Japanese military. Two,
that he never asked me for information about ourselves
and our life in camp. All he did was to stress repeatedly
that he was doing what he was doing because he was a
Christian and hoped that as a result of any services that
he might have rendered through me, he himself would
be excluded from the Allied retribution on the Japanese
that would follow their defeat (of which he appeared
to be as convinced as I myself was). This reassurance
I readily gave him.

The third factor was that he bore the endearing Kip-
ling name of Kim. I did not know at the time that there
are as many Kims in Korea as there are Smiths in Britain
or Joneses in Wales. In this tiny prison world of isolation and danger, it was extraordinary how one's
imagination, always in danger of drowning in the sense
of death and disaster which surrounded us, clutched at
straws. Ridiculous as it may sound, it was the coincidence that his name was the same as that of one of my

favourite characters in fiction, and that this character was known to all the multitudinous world of India as "Little friend of all the world," that perhaps more than anything else encouraged me to go on communicating with him to the end.

Towards the end of 1944 the whole tone as well as the content of Kim's communications with me began to show a new trend. He spoke of a great increase of tension at Japanese headquarters and a grimmer mood, as if secretly they were at last beginning to admit to themselves the possibility of a disastrous defeat. There was also, he said, a feeling of acute unease over the consequences of the growing spirit of nationalism among the indigenous peoples of the island, which they had done so much at one stage to encourage, and a marked coolness in their attitude to their chosen nationalist leaders like Sukarno and Hatta. Far from still regarding nationalism in Java as the powerful ally they had originally envisaged, they seemed to be thinking of it more and more as a force which might well turn against them and stab them in the back when the Allied attack on Southeast Asia began.

This suspicion had been sparked off by the mutiny in 1944 of a group of young Javanese officers who were being trained for military service by the Japanese at Blitar, in East Java, and the escape of the ringleaders of the revolt to the great hills on the south coast of the island where they were still at large.

I could not of course commit any of this information to paper, but much of what I learned from Kim at the

time was contained in a long dispatch I wrote for Lord
Mountbatten immediately after the Japanese capitulation, when my memory of these events was fresh and
clear. With the help of the notes I made for this dispatch, I recall vividly not only the change in the Japanese mood which he reported to me but also a somber
transformation in Kim himself.

He no longer mentioned any impending moves of
working parties from our depleted though still crowded
prison camps in Java to the outer islands, or of move-
ments from one camp to another within the islands, as
he had done before. He spoke as if communications by
sea between Indonesia and other parts of Southeast
Asia had ceased to exist, and as if the command in
Indonesia was more and more thinking of itself as condemned to fight on, completely isolated and alone,
against the Allied invasion when it came; to the usual
Japanese end, *without* surrender, of course, and to the
death of every man. Although he could give me no
complete details as yet, he made it clear that he viewed
the consequences, for all of us, of this change of mood
with growing fatalistic alarm.

Kim's own change of mood, which appeared to be
based at first on some as yet unacknowledged intuitive
appraisal of the change in the Japanese attitude to the
war, was for me the gravest portent of all. Up to now
his communications, even in the second- or third-hand
form in which they reached me, had an underlying
tone of optimism about the future, as if he believed that
the Japanese defeat was inevitable but also, unlike me,

that it would be a straightforward military matter which would be automatically followed by our and his own liberation.

For some months now there had been no cheerfulness, no optimism and no information of any tangible content except talk of these signs of growing Japanese desperation, and an atmosphere of fear of what might come out of this desperation. The fear at the back of Kim's mind did not emerge into the open and achieve an articulate form until a week or two after the final German surrender in May 1945.

It assumed then a definite warning that a new series of orders, which might have a fatal bearing on our survival, had arrived from the Japanese commander-in-chief in Southeast Asia. He did not know as yet what precisely the orders were, but, judging by the reactions all around him, they appeared to be orders of a grave and irrevocable import.

This commander-in-chief was a veteran Japanese soldier who had seen a great deal of active service, from the earliest days of the invasion of Manchuria and the subsequent wars in China proper. He was Field-Marshal Terauchi, a Japanese aristocrat of the oldest Japanese military school, a fanatical Imperialist of great independence of mind, impervious character, and with complete confidence in himself and in his own rightness of decision and behavior.

However grave the defeat of the Japanese navy and air force in the Pacific, however rapid the penetration of the American forces into the islands of the Sea of

Japan, despite the landing of the American armies in
the Philippines, the surrender of the Germans, the collapse of the armies in Burma and the advance on Rangoon of the British forces under Lord Mountbatten, he
utterly rejected, Kim said, any thought of defeat or
even peace by negotiation. He had made it quite clear
to all his subordinate commanders, in the various theaters of the vast strategic area under his command,
that they would be expected to resist the enemy in the
classical Samurai manner, if necessary committing
harakiri in the event of defeat rather than falling alive
into Allied hands.

This obviously sounded, to Kim as well as to myself,
like a prescription also for the death of all in the power
of the Japanese, because I myself could not see how
the Japanese would have any regard for the lives of
their prisoners at a moment when they had none for
their own.

If this were to be the way they were going to end
the war, then the process that I have called "the vengeance of history," at work like some volcano stirring
in the subterranean levels of their uncompromising
spirit, would logically demand the sacrifice of all the
thousands of the enemy races in their power.

My worst apprehensions were indeed quickened by
the first piece of concrete news from Kim to reach me
in June 1945. It was brief and to the point: the Japanese had decided to liquidate all their prisoner-of-
war camps on the coast of Java and to concentrate
them in the central plateau of the island at Bandoeng,

where we were originally held. Similar concentrations of *civilian* male prisoners were to be carried out simultaneously. Although Kim did not say so, I gathered from my Chinese friends that he thought this re-concentration an ominous sign.

The re-concentration was quickly and heartlessly carried out, and soon we were enclosed in what had been our first prisoner-of-war camp in Bandoeng, in such numbers that we could hardly move. In another old disused Dutch army barracks nearby, Dutch and Javanese civilian prisoners were held in even greater numbers than our own. We had never had much room in Japanese prisons, but the congestion that followed this re-concentration surpassed anything that even we, with our experience of the Japanese capacity for demanding the well-nigh impossible of us, could have conceived in a nightmare moment of imagination. In comparison with what was to happen, this was not congestion but life in wide open spaces—*Lebensraum* in the most expansive of Teutonic senses.

We had not been in this terrible over-congested state a fortnight when Kim's considered interpretation of the move reached me. It was what I had feared. He had had a glimpse of Field-Marshal Terauchi's secret order to his commanders. They laid down clearly that, when the Allies began their final assault in Southeast Asia, they were to kill all their prisoners in their camps, military as well as civilian, and fight to the classical Samurai end. I had barely come to terms with Kim's news when another warning from him came to tell me that we were about to be forced into even greater concentration, for what could well be the preliminary to final extinction.

Within a week we were marched out of our camp, somehow managing to keep in step and proper military formation. As always, when faced with the worst, our men somehow seemed to have some reserve of spirit left which made these miserable occasions a kind of carnival of self-respect and pride; something that I have always found far more moving than any surrendder to despair could possibly have been. But so near the end of our physical resources were we all, that I still see the long file of emaciated men walk the road of my memory in conditions that made the famous march at the beginning of the film *The Bridge on the River Kwai* seem by comparison a parade on the trooping of some royal colours.

On the outskirts of Bandoeng we were pressed into an even smaller prison, called the Lands-opvoedings-gesticht, soon to be renamed "Landsop" by the British soldier, with his genius for converting foreign sounds into convenient terms of his own. This prison was a sort of Borstal which the Dutch had built, both as a prison and a reformatory, before the war to hold approximately a hundred and twenty boys of criminal tendencies. Into these minute confines some seven thousand of us were somehow pushed and expected to live until whatever end to the war the Japanese had in mind.

The congestion was so great that even the Japanese

had to acknowledge that life inside it would be impossible unless our new prison were treated like the hold of some kind of ship. They provided us with rough timber, so that in every room we would build layers of wooden bunks on which we slept in narrow tiers from floor to ceiling. But perhaps the fact which illustrates best the density of our concentration is that the men stood in queues twenty-four hours a day all the time we were in this prison for their turn at the latrines, and we had to have on duty constantly a chain of officers and men passing buckets of water filled from an open irrigation ditch, which fortunately ran through the middle of our new camp, so that the latrines could be continually flushed with water. They did this so effectively that the latrines were almost the cleanest part of our prison. Had we not insisted on this as one of the most urgent of our self-imposed disciplines, I am certain we would have had epidemics of diseases that would quickly have deprived the Japanese of the necessity of inflicting on us the end which they more and more appeared to have in mind.

Despite the disorder caused by the move, my link with Kim still remained unbroken for some time longer because of two factors. First, the Chinese with whom he appeared to have such close contact in the world outside seemed to have a trusted representative among the persons who were still allowed to bring increasingly minute quantities of food to sell at the prison gates—unbelievable as this may sound to anyone without experience of the cupidity of our Korean guards and the urge of the under-paid Japanese prison staff to make money out of the commissions and bribes which they got for this pathetic traffic. Somehow, whenever there was anything of importance to impart, this person managed to pass it on to me through the young Royal Air Force officer who organized and supervised the purchase of food on our behalf. Without him this link could never have been maintained.

He was a Scot, Pilot-Officer Donaldson, and a person in whom I had complete confidence. I had met him on the first day of my release from my cell by the Japanese into a general prisoner-of-war camp, an occasion already some three years in the past. He was one of a small band of men under Nichols who had refused to join tamely in the general surrender to the Japanese ordered by the commander-in-chief of the Allied forces, General Ten Poorten. The General's own armies had not fired a single shot in resistance to the Japanese invasion. Only one battle had been fought on the island, and that was by the British, mostly Australians, aided by an American battery of the famous French 75 guns from Fort Worth. In the spirit which had prompted this stand against hopeless odds, Nichols and his men had made a determined effort to join me, and the Australians already with me in the jungles of the Sunda land, in the far west of the island. They had unfortunately run into a Japanese patrol on the way, and had had no option but to surrender. Treated as men in the Japanese category of "dangerous prisoners," they were thrust into the part of an old civilian prison, at a place called Soekaboemi, previously reserved by the Dutch for condemned criminals. There I was forced later to join them.

I do not know where in Scotland Donaldson was born, but he had the qualities of a Robert Louis Stevenson Highlander. He even looked the part. His build, for instance, was that of a man of the Bens, broad-shouldered, of medium height, immensely strong, as full of energy and temperament as Alan Breck ever was. He was good-looking in a truly Gaelic way, with thick black hair, blue eyes, and a fair complexion; he was absolutely fearless, a born buccaneer in the better sense of the word, and with an imagination and spirit which thrived on risk. Even if somewhat unpredictable at times, he was passionately loyal to those to whom he had committed his affections. Moreover, in the course of a long period of service in Malaya, he had had the imagination to see how important it was to learn to speak fluent Malay. This was, I believe, just another manifestation of his innate capacity for getting on with Oriental races of all kinds, from the over-sensitive Malays and Javanese to impossible Koreans and complicated Japanese.

He himself was too independent and complex a character to conform completely to service discipline and conditions, and was therefore never a favourite of senior service officers; but both Nichols and I liked him from the start. I trusted him implicitly, and realized that all the qualities which I have mentioned could make him an inspired smuggler. From the start

we had put him in command of our camp organization
for getting in food from the outside.

We appointed as his chief assistant a young American, who had left the United States soon after the outbreak of war to volunteer for service with the Royal
Air Force. He had come to Java as a pilot-officer in a
squadron of British Hurricanes. His name was Cicurel,
and he was a member of an ancient Egyptian-Jewish
family which had considerable commercial interests in
the Near East as well as in the United States of
America, to which his own branch of the family had
emigrated.

This temperamental but indomitable little man, who
at an early age had been water skiing champion of the
United States, seemed to have a natural genius for
barter and trade with the sharp-witted Oriental ped-
dlers of food with whom he and Donaldson had to
deal. But always under the handicap of having no
alternative sources of supply. It was a duty which demanded not only great skill but steady nerves and
great courage. Both Cicurel and Donaldson frequently
suffered at the hands of Koreans and Japanese, either
for incurring their displeasure at the successful way in
which they conducted the trading, or just because they
were in daily contact and therefore the most obvious
targets for any outbursts of spite, bad temper or anger
over news of the latest Allied atrocity invented by the
Japanese military propaganda machine. Nonetheless,
both these young men never failed us. They conducted
their part of the little trading allowed us with such skill

that, except during the periods of general punishment and fasting inflicted on us from time to time by the camp command, the system survived almost until the end of our captivity. Thanks particularly to Donaldson, who was able to help us later at great peril to himself in another acute crisis, I never lost contact with my Chinese friends outside.

There was one other inestimable link. We had in the camp a wealthy Batavia merchant who, for some reason neither he nor I could ever fathom (except perhaps a suspicion that his sympathies were with the Allies), had been put into a military prisoner-of-war camp. He was Mr. Tan: a small Chinese gentleman. Tiny even by the slight Javanese standards of physique, he was one of the most magnanimous and imperturbable spirits I have ever known. I cannot recollect *one* occasion, however grave, on which he appeared to be in the least put out or in danger of losing his dignity and calm. The respect in which he was held by everyone can be measured by the punctilious manner in which everyone, from the most senior officers to the humblest of privates, unfailingly addressed him—or even referred to him behind his back—as "Mr. Tan."

He it was who helped me organize the steady flow of money into the camp from the Chinese outside. He had his own subtle and highly effective system of contact with his friends who were still free. Both he and I thought it as well that I should not know about his contacts. To this day I have no clear picture in my mind of how he managed so detailed and reliable a system of contacts. Whenever the contacts through Donaldson failed, Mr. Tan invariably appeared and passed on to me, in impeccable Dutch, the latest information, often of the most crucial content, without any show of emotion, as if he were never anything more than a kind of radio announcer giving me the latest weather report.

Accordingly my contacts with Kim were maintained so well that, within a week or so of our re-settlement, a detailed message from him reached me that, unless some miracle intervened, a massacre of prisoners everywhere in Southeast Asia appeared inevitable.

One of the most difficult problems for me in life has always been to draw a distinction between fear and wishful thinking on the one hand and valid intuition on the other. Fears of the unknown future, I had already suspected long before the war, had an unfailing knack of passing themselves off as authentic apprehensions of the reality to come. The suspicion had become a conviction in war, painfully reinforced by the three years of prison experience behind me. There was no doubt in my own mind now, after this warning from Kim, that the most critical moment of our lives in prison was approaching, and that the drawing of a valid line between what was nothing but fear and what was an authentic sense of what lay round some dangerous corner of time (which is the function of intuition in the human spirit) was both more urgent and more difficult than ever. So, making use of all the experience and truth of which I was capable, I tried to reappraise these two elements, which seemed to be fighting a histrionic duel with each other for possession of my thinking at the time.

Despite Kim's fatalistic forebodings, and my own awareness of the perils to which "the vengeance of history," as well as orthodox Japanese military psychology exposed us, I came to no final conviction of disaster. Indeed I arrived at something almost as uncomfortable; a belief that no conclusion was as yet possible. Like Kim, I was full of fear of what *might* be our end. Yet still I could not find any clear intuition in myself that our fears would necessarily prove accurate. All that I possessed of intuition still prompted a belief that, as far as we were concerned, the issues of life and death were still being weighed in the balance, and that we would not know until the very last moment which of the two would be our fate.

I myself, paradoxically, took heart from this state of inconclusiveness, although it made the day- and night-long battle between fear and hope in me almost unbearable. Yet, whatever courage I derived from this continual tension, I felt compelled now to prepare as never before for the worst. I realized I had to assume that a massacre would take place, and plan without delay to resist it by whatever means we could. These means, considering our physical plight, the conditions of our confinement and the lack of arms of any kind, were pitiful to say the least. It was obvious to me that should the Japanese decide on a massacre, few of us, if any, could survive. The most one could hope to accomplish by resisting a general massacre would be to enable a few of us to escape in such confusion as we might create at the last moment, so that they could carry news of what had happened to us to our families and the world.

For the first time I took into my confidence others, whom I felt I could trust and who would best serve the purpose I had in mind. I picked first on a Royal Air Force squadron-leader, an officer who seemed to me fearless and physically almost immune to the consequences of years of malnutrition. He still appeared, if not as fit as at the beginning, far fitter than anybody else in the camp, and full of amazing energy. I told him then, under a pledge of secrecy even to his senior officers, all that I feared. I stressed even more to him than to myself that this was a fear and not an intuition, but nonetheless a possibility against which any commander should take every precaution of which he was capable.

The two of us together made a survey of all the men and officers in the camp, and drew up a list of some hundred and twenty British men who were not only the fittest we could find but men whom we could trust. We divided the camp into six sections and in each section picked the best possible platoon of twenty men, under the command of the fittest officer in the area. Even so, the security risk of sharing our full purpose with so many men thrown in daily contact with thousands of persons of so many different races and cultures was far too great to be run. Accordingly we did not tell them the truth but merely explained in the beginning that we wanted them to think of themselves as a kind of élite for the military police force we would need to help an orderly take-over from the Japanese in the confusion which we expected would follow surrender. We prepared them, through calm and measured discussion, to be ready day and night when summoned by the officer in command of their platoon to assemble in their part of the prison and await orders.

All this was easy to organize, but, comforting as it was to have some sort of plan in mind, the disconcerting fact remained that we were still a body of men who, however resolute, were completely without arms. There was not even any loose wood lying about in the prison for us to use as weapons should the Japanese decide to invade the camp in force to exterminate us. We could have decided, of course, to break up our wooden bunks and use the wood as quarter-staffs or our idea of Zulu knob-kerries, but the task of dismantling our beds would have taken so long that we would be shot down or bayonetted before we could do so in time for the purpose, since the hour of massacre, if it came, would undoubtedly come with little warning and at great speed.

Our strategy too, in the first instance, would obviously have to be kept behind the inner walls of our prison so that the Japanese could not use their machine guns on us. We would somehow have to induce them to come into the prison itself, where we would have a chance of engaging them in some kind of hand-to-hand combat. We dismissed it as unlikely that they would march us out of prison, because once out in the open they would need far greater forces for accomplishing their purpose; and even with such forces, opportunities for scattering and escaping would be greater for many more of us than if the Japanese did their work behind prison walls.

I had no doubt myself that, should they decide on the worst, they would favour the method most economical of their man-power because they would need every possible soldier they could muster for beating off the Allied attacks. There would have been no point otherwise in taking so much trouble to force us into our present terrible state of concentration.

We had therefore, happily, only the one main contingency to plan for—a final battle within the walls of the prison; and one great problem—finding arms for ourselves. The best way that occurred to me of solving the latter—we had no knives even, beyond a few used in the camp kitchen which was under close and constant supervision—was to obtain stones. I had seen stones used with devastating effect against armed police in Africa, as well as in communal riots in India. If we had an adequate supply of stones available in our camp, and provided we acted in such a manner that the Japanese and their Korean accessories were forced to enter the camp itself, I felt we would have some chance of overcoming some of them and capturing a few rifles and bayonets to help us in our resistance.

This chance would be all the greater because, provided we succeeded in keeping our plan a secret, the

Japanese, instead of surprising us, would themselves
be taken by surprise. From what I had seen of them
they were not particularly good in unexpected situations. Resourceful as they were in their planning, and
brave as they were in the execution of any precon-
ceived scheme, they tended to be at a loss when their
plans failed them. They tended to work rigidly by conscious rule, but when conscious rule vanished some
profound law of their spirit made them bunch in
moments of crisis. Indeed I had seen the unexpected
send them swarming in a kind of self-protective frame
like bees around a queen and held together there as if
in the vortex of what is perhaps the deepest and most
powerful collective sense of any nation in existence. A
surprise attack could well make them bunch, and once
bunched they would be extremely vulnerable to a
resolute and sustained stoning.

There is no point in going into the minute details of
all the plans, A, B, C, D, etc., which the two of us developed, or the various manners in which we intended
to launch and adapt the battle within the camp according to circumstances, because my only reason for mentioning the matter here is to use it as an illustration of
our desperate condition in our last prison, and the
sense of predetermined doom which was coming down
like the fall of a moonless night on the spirit of our
captors and those of their few forewarned captives.

But what is worth mentioning, perhaps for the same
reason, is how we obtained the stones. Unhappily
there *were* hardly any stones in the quadrangles of our

prison. I knew there were plenty outside, because I had seen them for myself on our march into camp. The problem was how to get them inside the camp, and fortunately here the weather came to my rescue. I think it was perhaps the rainiest of all the four Julys we experienced in prison. We seemed to have tremendous downpours almost every night, the rain so heavy that it transformed the great flashes of forked lightning—some looked a foot wide—darting through it from the vast towers of monsoon clouds raising their heads far above us in the night, I imagined, like a colossal complex of Hindu temples. Because of some mysterious process or refraction by the heavy raindrops, the lightning appeared to us a curious purple color, and would fill with a wonderful imperial light my own dark little world, contained within a single mosquito net suspended from the bunk above me and falling down to the stone floor on which I was trying to sleep. The thunder that followed always made for me the most wonderful music I have ever heard, because it became almost a divine voice resounding in my imagination with the most authoritative exhortation not to forget that, powerful as the Japanese were, there was a far greater power at work in the universe outside, which sooner or later would end their brief and brittle assumption of empire. I would awake at dawn refreshed, and go out to the roll call which began each day, to find the uneven surfaces of the prison quadrangle turned into pools of water.

The sight of these pools of water, one morning, suggested the answer to the problem of the stones which had become one of my major preoccupations. The Japanese throughout their occupation had shown themselves hypersensitive, if not profoundly afraid, for themselves, in matters of sickness and disease. It occurred to me that if the senior Dutch doctor—the Japanese had for centuries thought Dutch medicine the best in the world—could persuade the prison command that water in the camp not only would breed malarial mosquitoes but, through stagnation and pollution, cause other far more dread diseases like typhoid, the Japanese would respond to any preventive measures he might suggest. The measure I had in mind was that we should be allowed outside daily, and within the vicinity of our prison collect stones to level out the unevenness of the surfaces inside, and to camber them in such a way that any fall of water would be drained instantly into the main irrigation ditch which ran through our camp. The ruse worked. Every afternoon for several days we were energetically hustled out of the camp as if the Japanese had thought of the plan themselves, to collect stones around the prison and so liberally level out the surfaces within.

These afternoons were for me among the most unforgettable moments I spent in captivity. This feeling of growing peril which I cannot emphasize enough, combined with the stress of having to contain vital secrets and responsibilities almost alone, heightened my perceptions to what in hindsight appears to have been close to an extrasensory degree. I would walk out of the prison walls and feel that I had never, even in my childhood, seen the physical world with such intensity and known it to be so beautiful and so full of wonder. I would emerge from the purple shades of prison and pause by the gates to gaze at it for as long as I felt it wise—in order not to provoke the undesirable attention of the guards. I would pause, indeed, not only to take in the beauty of the scene beyond the walls but because so much and so profoundly had prison walls become a part of one's life that, on these extremely rare occasions when one was allowed to walk through them, one's senses reeled from the impact of a world without walls. It was almost as if walls had come to mean not just instruments of confinement but a physical support against the vast, free, comparatively empty and uncontained world outside. One seemed afraid that without walls for one's vision to lean on, one's spirit would not only totter but one would lose one's balance and, giddy, fall bodily to the ground. I was to learn, when talking to friends who had been in prison with me, later on when the subject was no longer too painful for public discussion, that they had for days after their release precisely the same sensation of being in danger of falling over without prison walls to support them. We were in this regard like men who had been forced to walk on crutches because of broken limbs for so long that they were afraid to abandon them weeks after they themselves were mended again, and for months would hanker to have their crutches back.

In addition to the heightening of perception of
which I have spoken, there was the stimulation of one's
senses provided by the extraordinary beauty of the
scene itself. For me there is no scene of greater beauty
on earth than this high plateau on which our prison
stood. Immediately behind us there was the great volcano of Tangkoeboehan-praauw, which is a Malay
name meaning literally "the ship turned upside down,"
because the shape of the mountain could, with the help
of a little poetic imagination, be visualized as a legend-
ary Malay ship turned upside down and petrified by
time; so much so that I often thought of it at night as a
symbol of our own state—for whose world could have
been turned more upside down than ours? All around
Tangkoeboehan-praauw, as far as one could see,
stretched great terraces of rice descending to a plain
full of the geometric shapes of more and more paddy
fields.

On these terraces and in these paddy fields one
would see the peasants of the island at work under
their wide-brimmed hats of golden rice-straw, in the
slow, patient, timeless manner of souls dedicated to
cultivating the earth, which always suggests that the
greatest and longest and most terrible of wars and the
most powerful of dynasties could come and go but
only the cultivator would be there to go on forever.
One would see, in one and the same moment, rice in
the full round of its processes of growth on earth. One
saw it being planted by hand in paddy fields filled with
water; one saw it standing lush, and of a green charged

with a kind of electricity which made it sparkle and crackle in front of one's eyes; one saw it a rich, golden colour standing tall, each head of rice bowed reverent with the weight of grain, and a line of women patiently harvesting it. Wherever a patch of water in the paddies showed itself to the sky, it revealed not only its own quicksilver surface but, as in a cool mirror, the profound reflection of the solemn topless towers of clouds that were building up in the blue sky for another downpour of rain at night.

In the heat of the afternoon the clear air of the island over this high plateau not only trembled from the impact of the long lances of bronze equatorial sun, but also vibrated with a strange, quick kind of rhythm which seemed to come to it from tomtoms beating deep down under the thin-skinned earth, mobilizing its tribal hordes of fire, lava and earthquake, for those colossal files of the volcanoes which bestrode the 690-mile-long island from west to east in twenty-league strides. I call it thin-skinned, because as earth goes the earth of Java is extremely young in geological time, and everything on the island still had upon it a kind of sheen like that of a new-born calf. It was still so sensitive to earthquake and eruption that I felt even as I lay with my ear on the stones of my prison floor at night that I could always hear the tribal forces of this primeval earth drumming barbaric below me.

To add to this tremble of air and light there were millions of dragonflies, with bodies as if made from some aluminium of stars, wings of slivers of sapphire so fine as to be transparent, and heads of turquoise, darting ceaselessly over the burning paddy waters, until the brilliant atmosphere became so sequined and crackling with such a quick electric sparkle and shivering with such a refined inter-vibration of precious wings that from time to time I would have to shut my eyes, conditioned to our motionless prison-shade, from it.

Finally, to frame this stirring canvas of our vision, in the far blue-satin west, as the perfect counterpoint to Tangkoeboehan-praauw, stood the other great mountain of the plain: Malabar—always a Hindu citadel, purple and imperial in the shadows cast from behind it by the long level light of the sinking sun.

What made this moment of beauty most poignant of all, perhaps, was that for people who had been so long in prison as ourselves it was an unchanging kind of beauty. It had been like that every day since we had been incarcerated. It had been like that because there were no seasons in Java: the jewelled land, from end to end, was like a long emerald strung on a shining cord of the equator itself and the climate seemed forever the same. There was no movement of winter into spring, spring into summer, summer into autumn and so on into winter again, to suggest that time ever changed and moved out of given moments of itself into other phases of change and renewal. One had never realized before how much one needed the seasons and how much one's own sense of renewal depended on their annual witness that not only life on earth but the universe itself was deeply and irrevocably committed to a process of greater becoming. This was the cruelty of the beauty of the scene, because it presented itself to tired and imperilled senses as evidence that time itself on this island might be on the side of the Japanese, and that the years of imprisonment would never change. There was for us, as it were, always only one day: there could only be another when we were free. It would take the nightly fall of rain, the purple lightning and the thunder to rescue me from this feeling of life in a trance from which perhaps now not freedom but death would release one. Fortunately there were the stones to gather and the irony of having to endure the bitter complaints of wornout, half-starved men, and officers not in the know, that one had done nothing to prevent the Japanese forcing them to this hard labour of collecting useless stones and carrying them back into our camp.

The ordeal, as these men regarded it, was over only too soon for me, because with so many thousands to collect stones the task was quickly accomplished and this precious world of infinite beauty was shut out from our eyes perhaps forever.

Once this was done, I arranged for each of the six platoons in their strategic distribution in the camp to maintain from them always a system of guards at night. Henceforth one man in each section was to be perpetually awake, listening for anything unusual in the sounds that reached the prison. Most of us, already some three and a half years behind prison walls, had developed an acute ability for interpreting the noises made by the guards on their rounds of duty, or those that drifted in from their quarters hard by the gates. For instance, on many occasions intimations of surprise searches for secret radios, hidden weapons or evidence of the plots that their imaginations, with all the fertility of the fanaticism which is a product of unacknowledged self-doubt, constantly imputed to us, had reached us through an indefinable awareness of a change in the tempo and timber of the sounds of Japanese activity from outside. This had happened in the middle of the night, in the early morning and even in the course of the prison day, and gave us just enough warning for the appropriate precautions to be taken. We now knew our captors so well, I felt, that we had only to be perpetually on guard to make it impossible for them to mount an action, on so great a scale as a massacre of some thousands of men would entail, without betraying it through sound or the abnormal absence of sound.

Even if our interpretation of the sound or its absence failed us, I had a conviction that we would know something of overwhelming import had reached the last stage of active preparation, through an intangible change of atmosphere that would forewarn and forearm us. I had often in the past seen dumb domestic animals in Africa so aware of the secret intent of the people who had bred and reared them and earned their trust that they could hardly walk, knowing they were being led to a distant place of slaughter. How much more, therefore, would not this same kind of subliminal mechanism, built into all living spirits, be accurately at work in us, who were in the power of men we mistrusted, provided we kept our minds open and awake to receive its warnings in the urgent code of our blood. From this time on until the end there was not a moment when there were not always seven of us perpetually at the ready to receive and perceive warnings of this or any other kind.

I say seven because I counted myself as an addition to the six. I have always, since I can remember, slept rather like an animal. I rarely sleep for more than a short period at a time and all through the night at brief intervals will find myself waking and sitting up to listen for anything unusual in the sounds of the night. I know that such a manner of sleeping is normally utterly unnecessary, at times most exhausting, and in the long run perhaps even harmful. Whether it is an inheritance from a family who lived for some centuries always on the dangerous frontiers of European expansion in Africa, or just a consequence of years of conditioning to some kind of continuing participation, even when asleep, in the changing manifestations of the nature of the aboriginal Africa I love, I do not know. All I can say is that I have never been able to change it and that, particularly all through my years in prison, however deeply involved I might be in a dream of sleep, I would be wide awake and listening at the slightest change in the rhythm or pull of the night.

All this done, there remained only the task of selecting the men who would have the greatest chance of escaping in the final hours, and carrying out the news of what had happened to us. It was obvious that none of us British could qualify for the role. Not only would our physical appearance give us away, however well we disguised ourselves, in an island so thickly populated with Javanese that it carried the densest proportion of persons per square mile of any area on earth; but our ignorance of the language, the people and the terrain would make it impossible for us to survive long enough to carry out so difficult a mission successfully.

It would need men who could pass themselves off as Indonesians of some kind, and so merge and blend safely in the world outside for long enough to meet the forces of liberation when they came. The only persons in these categories were obviously only to be found among the men under the command of the Dutch. The Dutch themselves, for all their knowledge of the country and the languages which most of them possessed, had the same physical disqualifications as we had. The most desirable candidates for the mission would have to be selected either from the few indigenous persons, or from Eurasians among their ranks.

Inevitable as this course of action was, it filled me with misgivings because we had already suffered severely in the past from the indiscretions of our fellow prisoners born and bred in the island, and their congenital incapacity for holding their tongues. Worse still, I knew that there were many informers and Japanese spies among the Eurasians who, incidentally, for many understandable reasons too long and complex to relate here, were among the most bitter and resentful men of mixed blood I have ever encountered on a wide beat around the world—a complete and surprising contrast to the warm, lovable, gay, intelligent, sensitive and responsive Cape-coloured people of my native South Africa.

I had already pinpointed some twelve of these Eurasian spies and informers. Of the twelve, there were two who made no secret even of the fact that they longed for a Japanese victory and who would do anything in prison to cultivate the favour of our captors and injure the Dutch. So dangerous were they that I, who spoke their language, made it my duty to try and break through their cold vengeful dispositions, and to keep some sort of human contact with them, as a form of insurance against the harm they tried to do. It was slow, hard and often distasteful work, but in the end some glow of fellow-feeling seemed to be stirring in them. On several occasions they deliberately shared with me information which they were about to pass on to the Japanese, and so enabled me to take preventive measures against the kind of reaction most likely from the latter.

So notorious and hated did the two become among the Dutch prisoners and their Ambonese and Menadonese soldiers in prison that, within a few days of our liberation, a Dutch officer came to my headquarters and confided to me that they had marched the two men out into the night and without trial of any kind shot them in the back. With such men about it was obvious how grave a security risk I would run in taking the Dutch command into my confidence and getting them to select the men we needed for our purpose.

I was certain that among the thousands of men in the Dutch part of our prison there were many persons as brave, reliable and true as any in our part of the camp, but the problem was how to find them; and once found, to get them to keep their own counsel. In this predicament I decided to consult my closest friend among the Dutch. I had many Dutch friends, because I was drawn to them not only for personal and historical reasons and spoke their language, but also because from the beginning Nichols had asked me to make the task of maintaining the closest liaison with them a special responsibility. Much of this work of course had to be done through the senior Dutch officers, and though there were many among them whom I respected, and with whom I had close personal bonds, the friendships that meant most to me were among the privates, junior officers and younger doctors under their command.

Indeed the person who meant most to me personally was a young Dutch lieutenant who the Japanese had insisted should be the principal interpreter in all our dealings with them. His name was Jongejans. He spoke fluent Japanese and, what was far more important, understood the Japanese better than most because his knowledge of them and their language was not a product of a mere cerebral study or academic curiosity but came out of a natural love of the Far East and its peoples. I think much of this was due to the fact that his own father had been a distinguished and imaginative Dutch administrator in Atjeh, a far northern province of Sumatra, the most difficult corner of the vast Dutch Empire, an area inhabited by a brave, fanatical and turbulent people, in constant revolt almost until the outbreak of war. Jongejans seemed to me to have inherited not only all his father's intelligence and interests but all his courage. He looked not unlike the young Van Gogh, had the same red hair, complexion and blue eyes charged with a sense of personal mission; though unlike Van Gogh his expression had a rounded proportion that betokened an unfailing sense of humour. Happily all his exceptional qualities were recognized after the war and he rose to, and still works in, the highest echelons of the Dutch Diplomatic Service. One of his last posts was that of ambassador to Peking, where he once more proved his courage and independence by refusing to give way to Red Guard pressures although confined to his embassy and cut off from the world for close on a year.

Like Nichols, he was constantly in touch with the Japanese command and always on hand as a convenient scape-goat for anything that went wrong; but neither his courage nor his sense of humour ever deserted him, so much so that he was one of the few Dutch officers in our prison to be honoured with a nickname by the British and Australian privates, erks and matelots. They called him "Zimmerzans" and to this day I encounter all over the world men who were in prison with me and ask me for news of "Zimmerzans."

I soon discovered that he and I saw the Japanese very much in the same light, and that in the difficult task of interpreting their actions and trying to anticipate the future he was the one man in prison whom I could consult with the certainty that nothing destructive would come out of the process and that my own thinking would invariably be the clearer for it.

I could not share my own secret burdens with him, because his own situation was only too vulnerable and his responsibilities heavy enough. For he was the strained link between the Japanese, who in the manner of the Oriental monarch who once cut off the head of the messenger who brought him bad news, always had an impulse to punish him for anything disagreeable which he had to impart, and the thousands of starving prisoners who, magnificent as they were, could not at times when things went wrong from their point of view resist a tendency to blame the system of our own command in which Jongejans played so vital a part.

He and I had already concluded that the end of the war was approaching fast. I knew too that, like me, he had no certainty as to the way it would end for us, although I deliberately abstained from going deeply into the matter. It was quite natural therefore for me to say to him that, in the confusion which we had to expect at the end, it would be as well to plan to have some men who could escape, in order to establish the earliest possible contact with the invading forces. I told him I believed that these messengers would have to be either indigenous persons or Eurasians. I was reassured that he not only welcomed the plan warmly but agreed that only Eurasians or indigenous men could carry out such a task with any prospect of success. For him too the most difficult aspect of the matter was how to pick four absolutely reliable men of this kind. He suggested that I should consult, not the Dutch Commanding Officer, but a Dutch colonel, a military engineer or sapper as we would have called him in the British army.

I was reassured by the fact that the officer Jongejans suggested I should consult was the person I had already provisionally in mind. He had come to us from another camp in the reconcentration of prisoners earlier in the year. I had not known him nearly as long as the senior Dutch officer in command, a warm, lovable person whom I liked as much as I feared his indiscretion, but I had taken to this Dutch sapper immediately and seen him regularly.

With this officer's help we selected one Menadonese, one Ambonese and two Dutch Eurasians, so dark that they could have passed for Javanese. I left him to instruct them in their mission on a warning from me, which I was determined to delay as long as was safe because of the security risk I have mentioned. I did not see the men myself and I did not tell the sapper colonel any more. I just helped him to accumulate a supply of civilian clothes and money for them. I left it entirely to the colonel to establish and maintain a special relationship with the chosen men from then on.

I cannot describe how much better I felt once the plan was complete, or how much the fact that we had some means of fighting back if necessary raised my spirits. I then had some of the best days and nights I can remember in prison until the last ten days of July 1945, when three things happened in quick succession. They showed that the final climax was very near, and that some of the vital aids on which I depended for a forewarning of Japanese reactions might fail me when most needed.

The first was that suddenly all contact with Kim and the Chinese outside ceased. Neither Donaldson and Mr. Tan, nor any of the various odd bodies in the working parties used outside the camp by the Japanese, who brought me scraps of useful information from time to time, could provide any clue as to why contacts that had survived so many different tests should suddenly have been broken. For days I faced the possibility in my own mind that they might have been detected and rounded up as suspects and could now be facing torture at the hands of the Kempetai, the all-powerful Japanese military secret police, who were such experts in all matters of torture that they invariably extracted any secrets from the most determined people in their hands. As the days went by however, and I myself was not sent for, I began to assume more and more that this last, and most dreaded of all explanations as far as I was concerned, seemed unlikely.

It could only be that the Japanese in Southeast Asia were expecting the ultimate invasion to be near and had put such unusually severe emergency measures into operation that our contacts had found that they could no longer function safely. This was confirmed by

the second of the three events I have mentioned. All
the Dutch and English senior officers were suddenly
summoned to parade one afternoon in the prison quadrangle. The summons, though extremely quick and unexpected, was not quick enough, I was happy to note,
to escape our system of early warning. I had time
enough to tell the Royal Air Force squadron-leader
who was my secret second-in-command to prepare to
alert his platoon officers for the plan we had evolved
for just such a contingency. But within a minute of being paraded I began to feel reassured that this, whatever it was going to be, was probably not the prelude
to massacre, because we were confronted only by the
strange and terrible Gunzo Mori, his satellite Kasayama, and the usual posse of excitable armed Korean
guards.

Mori had summoned us in a great rage because we
had refused to provide the Japanese command with a
list of names of any technicians among us who could
have helped them in the local armaments industry that
the Japanese had set up. We had pretended that there
were no such people among us, and the Japanese command, quite rightly, took us for liars. It was a striking
indication, even in this perverted form, of how instinctively the Japanese attached far more importance to
inner values than outer ones. A person's thought, and
his way of thinking, in a sense seemed always to matter
more to them than what a person did. We had at times
in the past been confined to our prison barracks without food and water for days because we were held

guilty of "wrong thinking." Ordered not even to con-
verse with one another, we were forced to sit behind
walls in silence so that we should contemplate the im-
perfections of our mind and spirit. Far back at the beginning, before I joined up with Nichols and his men,
I had even been condemned not so much for trying to
carry on the war against the Japanese but for having
shown "a spirit of wilfulness" in not obeying the orders
of General Ten Poorten to all the Allied forces under
his command and surrendering immediately to the
nearest Japanese military commander.

I had also on several occasions been beaten because
the vegetables I tried to grow in our various prison
camps, to augment our diet, were not growing fast
enough, or because the pigs which I tried to breed on
such swill as we could gather from the Japanese
kitchens and our own, in the hope that they might be a
valuable supplement of proteins to a diet dangerously
deficient in them, developed malnutrition afflictions of
their own, the sows casting still-born litters or just
dropping dead themselves from heart exhaustion. And
the cause of it all, according to the Japanese, had been
something "wrong in the spirit" that I brought to these
matters, never the lack of proper food or fertilizers.

Much of the rage to which we were exposed on this
occasion, I was certain therefore, was due to a sense of
perverted idealism in Mori and his assistants. In some
way, I suspected, he was seeing himself as an instrument of righteousness correcting a manifestation of
evil in us. I thought too that the rage was made all the

more dangerous because he was aware, as all the Japanese had been aware from the beginning, that however much they ruled our lives and had complete power over our bodies, they had utterly failed to change our mind and spirit. On the contrary, imprisonment in one way had improved the quality and texture of the spirit of our men and helped them to become finer instruments of life than they had ever been before. Somehow the Japanese were aware of this and could neither understand nor forgive us for it.

The parade had been called in such a hurry that we stood in line in haphazard order without regard to rank or seniority. I came about twelfth in the front rank of officers. The first officer in the line was a Battle of Britain pilot, Wing-Commander "Micky" MacGuire—still in the Royal Air Force today—knighted, an air-marshal and a senior member of the general staff of the combined British services. He had played no part in preparing the false return which was the ostensible cause of this Japanese outburst of indignation. But that fact did not spare him from being the first to be punished.

Being first, he was called out of the line and made to stand to attention in front of Mori, who at that moment looked to me like some Samurai character out of one of the "Noh" plays about to exact revenge for an outrage to his honour—a vastly popular theme of the classical Japanese theater, as I had noticed some twenty years before. His little sulphur satellite, Kasayama, with his usual ostentatious servility to his master, had

not forgotten, even in the haste with which the scene
had been set, to carry along with him a heavy wooden
armchair for Mori to sit in, should he wish to do so. But
Mori had ignored it.

He just stood beside the chair for some time screaming at MacGuire in the way the Japanese did when all
their emotions were most deeply engaged—the sound
coming not so much from their throats as from somewhere immediately behind their navels. He was using
words so fast and of so vulgar and crude a kind that I
recognized only a few of them, but enough to follow
the accelerating drift of passion in them. At the same
time his hand would repeatedly go to the hilt of the
sword at his hip as if he were tempted to draw it and
do away with MacGuire on the spot.

In the end it was not the sword but the wooden
chair that he chose as his weapon. He suddenly bent
down and lifted the chair from the ground. Small as he
was, he was broad-shouldered and immensely strong.
He raised it high into the air and brought it down with
such force on the head of the tall, emaciated Mac-
Guire, who even at the best of times was a slender person, that the chair was shattered. MacGuire was left
tottering and dazed, fighting with all his determination
and courage (of which he had more than most men) to
stay upright on his feet. Even this was not enough for
Mori, because he then proceeded to hit MacGuire with
his fists and kick him with his jack-booted feet before
pushing him, weak and in a state of profound shock,
back to join our line.

He then called out the officer next to MacGuire and each officer in turn was beaten up, both with fists and a piece of the shattered chair, with Kasayama now joining in more and more with kicks to help the punishment along. This to me, still unbeaten, and trying to appraise the situation and its full potential of consequences for us, was one of the worst moments of the afternoon, because I knew, as no one else in the camp did, how this powerful collective sense of the Japanese and their converts, which I have already mentioned, tended to take over in such situations. For instance, even on lesser occasions when we had been slapped and beaten for minor offenses, every other guard or soldier on duty had somehow felt compelled, as if by some instinctive sense of honour, to join the beating in their turn and show their solidarity of spirit as a Russian Marxist would have had it. I could visualize that before long the rest of the guard, already on the verge of flocking to Mori, might join in unbidden, but worse still, for the first time in years I saw a machine gun being mounted at the gates. I began to wonder if my interpretation of the cause of the parade had not been too naive and that this might not be just a pretext for the ultimate solution I had feared.

Still in a turmoil of doubt and wondering what I should do to resolve the crisis, my turn came to face Mori. I walked towards him suddenly feeling strangely calm. It was as if I had become another person and somewhere far down within me, someone far wiser and with the benefit of having had to face this kind of thing ever since the beginning of man on earth, took command of me. I faced Mori, and this other self gauged Mori's blows and anticipated his kicks so accurately that it was able to make me move my head and body at the last moment before the blows and kicks fell in a manner not perceptible to the enraged man and his satellites, yet sufficient to rob them of their severity— to such an extent that I hardly felt them.

Indeed the physical impact of what Mori was trying to do to me seemed so irrelevant that, during the whole time of his assault on me, this process within me of appraising the full meaning of the incident and searching my imagination for a way of putting an end to it all before it developed into something worse, even something which Mori himself might possibly not have intended, went on unimpeded, and if possible, with greater clarity than before. The result was that, when Mori delivered his final kick and pushed me back to my place in the line and I once more caught a glimpse of the machine gun at the gates, it was as if I heard from deep within myself very clearly a voice of command from this other self, ordering me as with the authority of life itself: "Turn about! Go back and present yourself to Mori for another beating."

Rationally, everything was against such a course of action. If there were normally anything which provoked the Japanese to extremes of punishment it was any action on our part that broke their rules and sense of order. Yet this voice that rang out almost like a bell within me was so clear and insistent that I turned about without hesitation, walked back and once more stood to attention in front of Mori before the next officer could take my place.

Mori was already in a position to beat up his next victim. He was on the point of attacking again when the realization came to him that he was being confronted with the very person whom he had beaten just a moment before. The shock of this slight variation in a process which he had taken for granted was great, and showed immediately in his eyes. He looked at me over his raised cudgel, arrested in its downward move, as a cliché would have it, like someone who was seeing a ghost in broad daylight. Indeed, so grave was the shock that it utterly broke up the accelerating rhythm of passion and anger in which he had been imprisoned. Slight as the irregularity was, it began drawing him out of the preconditioned processes of collective and instinctive reaction in which he had been involved and made him, I believe, suddenly aware of himself as an individual facing not an abstract and symbolic entity but another individual being. He stood there glaring at me, a strange inner bewilderment at this unexpected turn of events showing in the somber glow of his dark eyes. Then, taking another sort of half-hearted swipe at my head, he grumbled with a kind of disgust that he thought the whole matter utterly incomprehensible and beneath contempt. He gave me a shove in the direction of our line, turned about, and still muttering tersely to himself walked away and out of sight, Kasayama at his heels. We were left standing there until late that night, when Nichols and Jongejans, catching a glimpse of the Japanese lieutenant in command of our camp through a lighted window in his office, risked breaking ranks and, going to him, unorthodox and dangerously provocative as it was, got permission at last for us to dismiss.

Thinking it all over for hours that night in my own private little world underneath my mosquito net, I came to the conclusion that the afternoon's scene could not have happened six weeks before, and that it was in its own way slight—slight by our prison standards—evidence of the tension mounting in the Japanese military spirit—evidence perhaps of what the new mysteriously silent Kim had warned me; ominous testimony that the Japanese were near to breaking through such restraints as had governed them in our treatment up till then. The whole incident that afternoon could have been a slight instinctive dress-rehearsal for the final parade, the ultimate cataclysmic phase of our time in prison.

The third and most serious of the three things to alarm me was that, within a few days of Mori's outburst, our secret radio packed up and we had no means of telling what was happening outside. Although Nichols and I had from the beginning realized, I had thought to the full, the importance of knowing by radio how the war was progressing, I had not until that moment appreciated its overwhelming necessity to us.

We knew that the war in the Pacific and Burma was

very close to its climax. We knew all about the fall of
Okinawa and Rangoon, and the invasion of the Philippines. Above all we had listened to a program on the
effects of the American and British submarine war
against Japan, which had ended with the staggering
conclusion that in two years alone some four million
more tons of Japanese merchant shipping had been
sunk than Japan had been able to replace: that the
far-flung and widespread Japanese armies were for all
practical purposes cut off from their home bases and
main sources of supply, and that the overcrowded
main island of Japan itself must be near the beginning
of a process of slow starvation.

Yet nothing we had heard up to the moment our
radio gave out had suggested that the Japanese home
government was even thinking of ending the war by
negotiation or, more vital as far as we were concerned,
that their commanders-in-chief, supreme and independent overlords in their various theaters of war, had any
intention other than that of fighting to their and our
end.

News, like the detailed reports we had heard of the
Kamikaze pilots who crashed their planes loaded with
bombs into American ships of war and transports,
despite the most formidable barrages of anti-aircraft
fire warships had ever been able to mount, was proof to
me of how accurate had been my reading of the dangers implicit in the Japanese attitude to this war. Even
in time of peace I had been amazed by the vast extent
to which Japanese, of all sorts and conditions of so-

ciety, tended to idealize death at the expense of life. In some mysterious but extremely profound fashion, the way a person died seemed to be almost more important to them than the way he lived. It was almost as if, on balance, they despised life in the here and now. Their real romance often seemed concerned less with living than with dying and with death. Below the Bhuddist layers of their national culture, there was firmly embedded in their Shinto form of ancestor worship the myth of their direct descent from Ama-Terasu, the goddess of the sun. Yet it was not the day which ruled their imagination, I suspected. Their secret minds turned with infinite longing to the night, where their hearts were governed by the moon. The tides of instinct and feeling in the blood always seemed to me pulled by some inner moon of their unlived selves into action in their own lives, as the great tides of the Pacific Ocean were pulled high up and down their island shores by the outer moon they praised continually in paint, word and music. What they themselves regarded as the great triumph of the individual, my reading of their history and their literature told me, seemed to be inverted disaster. So often, triumph of the spirit for them was to be found, not in a victory over an enemy so much as in a noble acceptance of unjust defeat, and in overcoming its shame with self-inflicted death.

This was one of the many reasons why I had always felt, no matter how grim the news for us at the beginning, that the war could only end in defeat of the Jap-

anese because I was certain that, however glittering
the promises of their military day appeared to be in the
Pacific and Southeast Asia, underneath in the night of
their spirit, a secret unrealized self would be drawing
the tide of all their unacknowledged longing produced
by thousands of years of the secluded island history
which had conditioned their national psychology, to
find fulfilment only in utter defeat. It would do this I
felt certain, as irrevocably as the moon drew the waters
of the Pacific to those phenomenal neap-tides which so
often lapped at the brim of their vibrant land.

Their main inspiration as a people it seemed to me
had always welled up from the depths of cataclysm
and disaster of fire, water, earthquake, tidal wave and
typhoon. I suspected that, unknown to themselves, this
war was perhaps another and greater instinctive search
for renewal by destroying a past they could not escape
in any other way, through the disaster of utter collective defeat. Indeed the manner in which Japan has
come out of the disaster of the war and made itself into
one of the most formidable modern technological nations on earth, today seems to me to confirm that there
was some truth in these conclusions reached in the isolation of prison.

It can be imagined how these and many other similar considerations sharpened my feelings of desperation over the breakdown of our radio contact with the
outside world and made me, and the little group of
gifted and gallant officers concerned, search desperately for a means of putting it right. I suspected that

among the new groups of prisoners who had come into the camp on our re-concentration there was at least one if not two secret radios at work. I was reasonably sure that I knew the group of young Dutch officers responsible for one radio. I was sure I had only to ask one of them and I would probably get all the information we needed. One of the officers had become rather a friend of mine, although I had not known him long.

He was in many ways one of the most colourful characters among the thousands in our midst, a born cavalier, good-looking, debonair, gay, reckless, without fear but also passionately loyal in his friendships. Due, perhaps, to the fact that he had a great deal of Arab blood in his veins, he also possessed a natural gift for intrigue against his enemies that amounted almost to genius, preferably intrigue of the more dangerous kinds. His name was Max al Kahdri. He was a professional officer in the Dutch army and one of the younger of the numerous sons of the polygamous Sultan of Pontianak, on the island of Borneo. As a younger son, considered far removed from any possibility of succession, his father had washed his hands of him, as it were, by sending him to Holland to train for a modest career in the Dutch colonial army. He and I did not know at the time that the Japanese had already massacred his father and his wives and concubines, as well as some two hundred members of his family in Pontianak, and that on liberation he would find himself the sole family survivor and the new Sultan of his people.

I was certain that I had only to ask al Kahdri and he would give me the information I wanted. But I was determined to do this only as a last resort, because I had what seemed to me at the time good reason to believe that he and his group were under suspicion and were being closely watched by the Japanese. I knew this from the things said to me by the two Eurasian spies whom I have mentioned, and who had for some weeks now, whenever we met, somehow brought al Kahdri into our conversation. Being unaware, as al Kahdri also was, that his family had been massacred because the Japanese had accused the Sultan of intriguing against them, I could not take that sinister fact into consideration as I would have done. The Japanese may well have thought that some rumours of the massacre could have reached al Kahdri, even in their closely guarded prison, and their guilty consciences accordingly prompted them to suspect him of plotting against them in a bitter spirit of revenge. However, knowing none of this at the time, I thought he could only be being specially watched because of some suspicion that he was operating a secret radio. Under our physical conditions secrecy had become almost impossible, quite apart from the notorious incapacity of the people among whom his group operated to keep secrets even of the most vital kind.

So I put all thought of going to Max al Kahdri aside as the last possible resort. I limited my own association with him and his friends, all of whom I liked immensely, to such obvious and innocuous contacts that

I was to discover later that they had been secretly hurt by my attitude. Thinking I did not trust them, they had cancelled the decision they had already unanimously taken to confide in me.

Much as I regretted this, I still believe my action was right and that if I had become involved with al Kahdri and his group I might well have brought disaster upon them and myself. Besides, there was what appeared to be at the time a possibility of putting our own secret radio right ourselves. One of what were in those days called "acorn" valves and a small electronic condenser in the set had given out. We had no replacements for them. These acorn valves had been brought into our camp by an American Air Force officer some two years before. They were the latest thing in radio, and had enabled us to reduce the size of our set over the years to such minute proportions that we could conceal it in a pair of wooden clogs.

Most of us had been wearing clogs in prison because, over the years, shoes as well as the leather to repair them had progressively given out and we had been reduced to using wood and rubber to replace them. These special wireless clogs were slightly bigger and thicker than normal, but not so big as to attract notice. They were in any case a great and sophisticated improvement on our first set, which had been built into the seat of a wooden chair.

We had known from the start that the chair could only be a provisional home for a secret radio. In the first place, if we were moved suddenly we obviously could not take a large wooden chair with us. We had to have as soon as possible a mobile form of radio. Also we did not think a hiding place in a chair could long escape detection. The point was forcefully driven home to us one day early on when, during the course of one of their blitz searches of the camp, the Japanese sergeant-major in charge chose this very chair to sit upon while conducting the operation. Two of the officers responsible for the set, watching him bounding up and down in the chair, nearly had heart attacks because they were convinced that sooner or later the hollow sound each bounce emitted would draw his attention to the real role of the chair in our camp!

I need not describe all the stages of evolution which followed until we arrived at the solution of housing the set in the clogs and henceforth, whenever we had a blitz search, one of us could wear the clogs and walk about in them throughout the search, feeling on the whole safe from detection.

The forms of detection that we really feared most were those that could come through loose talk from the small circle in the know, or being caught out during the hours of listening in at night, when of course we were most vulnerable as the set then had to be extracted and exposed. If only we could now replace the damaged parts, or find other equivalents of the same size, we could operate the radio once more. The gifted young New Zealand officer—a radio expert in civilian life— who had been responsible for reducing the set to its final minute form, and had proved himself capable of

operating it for some eighteen months without any loss
of nerve and with a real if strange enjoyment which I
could not share—had impressed upon me how little he
needed either to make the set operative again or to
build a new one. But where and how were we to get
even so little in the most difficult, bleak, isolated and
impoverished prison we had ever encountered?

Donaldson, who was in the know, thought he had an
answer. The Japanese lieutenant commanding the
camp at the time had, among his own private supply
of loot from the world outside, one of the most luxurious and up-to-date radiograms. It stood in a room leading off from his office, where he went from time to time
to inspect his horde of treasure ready for shipping
home on the day of the victory he confidently expected. He either had one of the most fastidious senses
of property in existence or such a pride in maintaining
what were obviously also prestige symbols of the
highest value to him (like the large refrigerator and
of course the gramophone in his store), that he was
continuously calling on us to provide technicians to
examine them and make quite certain that they were
still in good working order.

Donaldson himself, who came from a Royal Air
Force unit of signals and knew something about these
things, was his favourite choice. I have already mentioned how valuable Donaldson's gift for getting on
with the different peoples of Southeast Asia, and in
particular with the Japanese, had been to us. It was
never of greater value than now. In the course of dis-

cussing with him what we needed to put the radio right he said at once, without hesitation:

"Why, it's very simple, I can get all these things from the camp commander's radiogram."

I remember demurring and saying something to the effect that if he extracted the parts from the gramophone and it did not work at all when next the Japanese commander tried it out, even the Japanese, ignorant as they were in technological things that a Western schoolboy would take for granted, could not fail to discover that some vital parts were missing. Their suspicions, already quickened to a degree we had never experienced before, would erupt, and the camp would be subjected to searches even more intensive than any we had yet known.

Even if they did not discover the missing parts, I dreaded far more what they might uncover in the rest of the camp, quite apart from Max al Kahdri's secret radio and the other instrument I suspected of being worked by other recent arrivals in our midst. I thought such a search could well have consequences far more dangerous to us than the lack of news of how the war was going.

I would have preferred going to al Kahdri and asking him to supply us with the information we needed, but Donaldson replied to my doubts that he would not be such a fool as to remove the parts we needed from the gramophone without replacing them with our faulty ones. He would merely, he said with another schoolboy grin, "effect an entry"—as the British police

term burglary—into the camp commander's office and
when he was sent for, as no doubt one day he would
be, by the Japanese commander, he would carefully
examine the gramophone and if necessary persuade
the commander that some of its parts had deteriorated
and needed replacement, and get him to obtain them
from the world outside.

This thought obviously pleased Donaldson immensely because I remember his smile of schoolboy
mischief and his saying: "That way we will not only
please the lieutenant but make certain that we have
another supply available in case our set goes wrong
again."

So one night the three of us, the New Zealander I
have mentioned, Donaldson and I, crept out of our
mosquito nets. Donaldson's net was next to mine, the
New Zealander's was in the corner farthest away but
nearer the gates of the camp. His role was to sit at the
entrance to the quarters with his feet in a basin of
water as if he could no longer endure the pain of neuritis which malnutrition had inflicted on so many of us.

This consequence of malnutrition was known to the
troops as "burning feet." It could be so painful that one
often saw men kept awake by it sitting all night long
with their feet in cold water in order to relieve the
pain. The sight of the New Zealand officer in this position therefore would not have struck any passing
guard as unusual. In his position nearest to the gates
his particular task was to listen for sounds of any night
patrol gathering to enter the camp. Should that hap-

pen, he was immediately to get up and walk towards the latrines, pass by me and tap me on the shoulder and then go on to join the twenty-four-hour queue patiently waiting their turn at the far end of the camp.

I myself was to stand in the shadows of the wall immediately outside the room which housed the camp commander's trove of loot. I had arranged that, in case of danger, I would tap three times on the windowpane and Donaldson would remain hiding in the room until I rapped three times on the pane again. I myself, having given him the first warning, meanwhile would do what the New Zealand officer had done and join the queue outside the latrines until the danger had passed. Should there be a surprise night search and the whole camp be turned out of their barracks I had undertaken to get the whole group of officers within my room to flock and mill around the incriminating windows, and so provide a screen for Donaldson to come through without being detected by the guard.

There were obvious snags in all these arrangements but it was the best that we could do. To Donaldson's and my amazement we found the window to the room unlatched. Donaldson raised the window silently, as if he had been a professional burglar all his life, went through it, closed it as silently and vanished from sight.

He was gone for close on half an hour I think, and it was a long, long half hour indeed. At first the camp was so silent that I heard nothing but the news of the natural world without: frogs croaking, not in the Greek fashion like the fateful "brek-ke-kex-kex" of Aristophanes, but in the Sanskrit, the original language of the myths and legends that dominate the Javanese imagination to this day, and which was inherited by the islanders some thousands of years before from their Hindu conquerors, the creators of the vast vanished Empire of Modjopait.

By the irrigation ditch I saw the fireflies come and go in the darkness, like stars through a muslin midnight mist. Above me a shooting star appeared and sank slowly and solemnly down towards the east, on one of the longest arcs of red light I have ever seen, before it too was extinguished. Down in the plains below from time to time I could hear plainly the nightwatchman, on duty at the entrance to his frail hamlet of wood and thatch, beat beside some star-filled paddy water a message of "all is well" on the large hollow bamboo gongs used for this purpose. After a while, fainter and further away, I would hear another neighbouring hamlet reply in kind. Indeed nothing could have sounded more peaceful and reassuring and yet the sense of the danger of what we were doing was so acute in me that I found no comfort in it.

I must have been standing there for some twenty minutes, the tension in me mounting, wondering why Donaldson should take so long—although he had warned me that, working in the dark at so complicated a machine, he would inevitably need time—when suddenly the noise of a car approaching the gates at great speed broke the silence. The car drew up at the gates abruptly, the brakes screaming from the friction of the speed at which they had been applied.

A loud "Kerrei!"—Attention!—rang out from the guard commanders.

I heard the guards tumbling out hurriedly, forming up outside the gates and slapping the butts of their rifles as they came to attention. This sort of thing had happened before and could mean that either the camp commander had arrived for a perfunctory inspection of his guard to satisfy himself that they were doing their duty or for a blitz search of the camp. On this occasion I immediately feared the worst. At any moment I expected the New Zealand officer, who was in a position to hear and interpret the detail of sound that followed better than I could, to appear and tap me on the shoulder; and then to see Donaldson, who must have heard the sounds as clearly as I did, and was in the most vulnerable position of all, coming through the window with his work uncompleted.

But neither the New Zealand officer nor Donaldson lost their nerve. Both remained at their respective posts and although a great deal of muffled sound and shuffling still went on in the guard room and voices continued chattering by the gates, the gates themselves remained shut. Ten minutes later there was a slight tap at the window, the window was silently raised and Donaldson climbed through it quickly, shut it as silently, and together we walked off in the direction of the latrines.

As we walked towards the queue of waiting men I could tell how great the tension had been for Donaldson because the news he had to communicate to me in a whisper came out of him like an explosion of breath from a person who had dived deep into dangerous water and had been forced to hold his breath for too long.

"I've done her, the bitch, Colonel!" he gasped. "I've done the bitch! We've got all we need!" We had hardly reached the queue when a night patrol entered the gates.

The next night the New Zealand officer, in the dark underneath his mosquito net, began to repair or rather re-shape our radio. It was difficult, delicate and slow work, and if I remember rightly it took three nights and three dawns to give him the necessary light before the work was finished. They were among the longest days I have ever known, because everything in the atmosphere around us told us that the climax was near. Also, quite apart from the change in the atmosphere, I could not explain Kim's failure to communicate with me nor the inability of the subtle, imperturbable and infinitely resourceful Mr. Tan to get news of his and my friends outside in other ways.

I was particularly aware at night of how time dragged on at this moment, and how great was the strain. I always went at night before lights-out to one or two of the sections of the prison in which our men were housed. The Japanese still insisted on keeping officers and men on the whole in separate quarters. I did this nightly round, not out of a sense of duty nor just out of the affection I felt for the men who had shared the long years of captivity with us, but also for the purely selfish motive that I had never yet gone among them without being revived and strengthened by my contact with them.

Great as was my admiration for the British officers in prison with us, it could not be compared with the respect I had for the ordinary soldiers, sailors and airmen who formed the majority of British prisoners. They seemed to me, even in the categories from which one might have least expected them, to possess qualities of the highest order. For instance, men from the slums of the great cities of Britain like London, Birmingham, Glasgow and Liverpool, whose physical appearance often showed the consequences of severe malnutrition during the years of their neglect by the ruling classes before the war, like the rickets of childhood which gave them bowed legs and Rowlandson bodies and faces.

Yet their spirit was always high, cheerful and invincible. I had never yet known a crisis, however brutal, in which they had lost their nerve. Appeals to their pride and honour had never been in vain. Always they had responded instinctively in a measure as great if not greater than officers born, bred, well-nourished from childhood, schooled and trained for precisely this sort of trial. Their need of honour, of a life of self-respect too, was as important as their need of food. They were, as I said in the beginning, all slowly dying from lack of food at the time, but there was no hint of impending

death in their conversation or sign of defeat in their
emaciated faces. Instead there was only an extraordinary and intense kind of gaiety that to me was far
more moving than any signs of depression, melancholy or defeat could possibly have been.

Talking to them I would find myself assailed by a
fierce kind of tenderness for them, that was like fire. I
wonder if anyone, except perhaps Wilfred Owen, has
ever paid enough attention to this kind of male tenderness that men feel for flesh and blood in war, not even
exclusively flesh and blood of their own kin but also of
their enemy. It is so perhaps, because the British have
this ridiculous feeling of embarrassment when faced
with emotion and feeling, of which they have such
great and sensitive reserves themselves. Any open acceptance of either, however, tended to be discouraged
as if it were a kind of un-masculine weakness. Yet it is
a unique reality of war, and not being British I was
open to it—much to the embarrassment of my more
conventional fellow officers at times. I had no inhibi-
tions in encouraging and welcoming it, but felt im-
measurably strengthened by it always to do what I felt
I had to do.

I would go back after these visits to my own mosquito net, both uplifted by my nightly contact with
such men and aflame with determination somehow to
protect them and with a re-glimmering of hope, despite the odds and the evidence, that I might still be
able to help to achieve this. By daylight, and in the
course of the exacting prison days that followed, these

feelings would be overlain by routine duties but would never utterly vanish. I only had to resume my rounds again at night to find it there, flaring up again like coals blown into the fiercest of flames.

I remembered too that in the course of these three long days, getting up as I always did every day long before roll call so that I could wash and shave myself before facing the Japanese, I would watch the moon, which in that sky before a dawn, clear as crystal-water after the rain of the evening before, was almost as magical as it is in Japan. The moon I noticed then was rapidly on the wane. At the end of that long night during which our radio was fully repaired again, it rose in its last phase of waning just before the sunrise, with Venus as morning star ahead of it. The planet looked so large and of such an abundant liquid clarity that I felt, if I held my hands cupped out towards it, they would be filled and overflowing with its lovely light. It may sound unduly superstitious, but watching the moon in its last phase, I thought it as much a portent as the soothsayer did Halley's comet, when he warned Shakespeare's Julius Caesar to beware the Ides of March. It seemed no idle coincidence to me that the moon, which plays the great symbolic role in the movement of the Japanese spirit that I have stressed so much, should be in the last phase of dying just when the end for the Japanese in this war appeared to have drawn so near.

The day that followed was one of the longest of all. It was singularly quiet. No call for working parties came from the Japanese and no traders appeared at the prison gate. Both the Dutch and British commanders who reported at the Japanese camp commander's office for the daily meeting, the "Tenko," as the Japanese called it, were sent back by an unusually subdued and quiet Gunzo Mori with the abrupt comment that they were not needed.

Jongejans, who had been kept behind for a discussion of various routine affairs, also returned to tell me later that the camp commander had not even put in an appearance at his office. He himself had never known our captors quite so still, subdued, indifferent to us, as if they were all inwardly profoundly preoccupied.

As always on these occasions, the men gathered together to pursue their studies in the various classes which we had organized for them, and maintained unfailingly whatever the conditions and temporary interruptions, throughout more than three years of imprisonment. With no working parties out of the camp, the classes had not been so well attended for months.

One of the several classes which I myself conducted was a course in Japanese. I think it is a significant illustration of the triumph of our men over the resentment one might have expected them to have on account of their brutal treatment, that it was one of the most popular classes of all. I saw many faces there that day which I had not seen for some weeks—in fact so great was the attendance that we only managed to squeeze into a part of one of the men's quarters where I sat on a bunk totally surrounded.

The men as usual sat attentive, making their notes on the only paper we possessed—the lavatory paper with which the Japanese daily supplied us with a strange generosity, so unlike their meanness in other and far more vital issues. This paper was so precious that it was never used for the purpose for which it was intended, but reserved for such important uses, as for instance, the writing of our own textbooks (which we had to do, having no libraries) and making notebooks for the thousands of men who were re-educating themselves through these classes.

On this particular day my Japanese class was an oddly happy occasion because, apart from a conventional study of Japanese grammar and syntax, it ended with a general discussion of Japanese literature and in particular of an aspect of it which had many happy associations for me. It was an account of the sustained rivalry between Murasaki-San, the lady of the Imperial Court who wrote the great *Tale of Genji*—the Genji-Momotari—and Shei Shonogun, the author of the witty and malicious *Pillow Book*.

Both of them were brilliantly translated by Arthur Waley, whom I had known as a boy in London and who had been responsible for introducing me to the world of Bloomsbury when it was in full and strange flower, as rarefied almost as Shei-Shonogun's world had been. I told them about the unreal, delicately over-aesthetic life the ladies and their lovers led in Kyoto, the exquisite parties they gave in some lacquered pavilion in one of the thousand and one gardens of the beautiful old capital of Japan, which contained, each in its own unique fashion, as in a jewelled miniature, all that the Japanese thought was of beauty and proportion in the wider world.

I told them above all of the paradox implicit in the behavior of these inspired ladies and their elegantly effete friends who could make one of the highest priorities of their spirit just watching the moon rise and throw its own yellow Chinese script on the precious little streams which always figured at the center of these secluded scenes. The ruthlessness of all aesthetes has always impressed me more than their sensitivity and these hypersensitive lovers of selective arts were no exception. They sat in these still, microcosmic gardens, the moonlight a kimono of silk about them, impervious and unheeding of the grim realities of the civil wars of their day, not only making appreciation of the sort of special beauty in which they were taking delight impossible, but also creating an ugly waste in the physical scene as well as in the mind of the larger world without. It was most strange how even in this class the moon had insisted on intruding at the end.

But one of the strange events of the day came after the class, as I was walking back to my own part of the camp. I had to pass near the Japanese lieutenant's office and the window which Donaldson had so expertly forced some three nights before. As I did so I was startled suddenly to hear the gramophone record which was being broadcast on the camp radio. It shook my senses almost as the moment which shook T. S.

Eliot's memory, as he puts it in one of his greatest poems, "Like a madman shakes a dead geranium."

To this day I believe that if Hollywood were to make a film of our imprisonment under the Japanese and were to include this moment and this record in it, it would be condemned universally for what old-fashioned critics used to call "laying it on with a trowel." The gramophone was playing a record of Yvonne Printemps singing "I'll follow my secret heart." I had heard other tunes on the Japanese camp radio broadcast from time to time, full of personal associations for me, but none quite so evocative as this nor so relevant and pertinent a comment on my own life in camp. The pertinence was obvious, only the evocation needs explanation. Briefly it was of London in the 'thirties and in particular of the occasion when I took a great friend of mine, Lilian Bowes-Lyon, the poet, to the first night of a musical play by Noël Coward called *Conversation Piece*, to see and hear Yvonne Printemps herself in the lead, singing this very song.

Finally, at the end of this longest of long days there was a magnificent sunset of the kind I had always as a boy in Africa described to myself as a twilight-of-the-Gods prelude. The nightly fall of rain somehow had been retarded and towards the west there was a deep valley of the bluest skies between two Himalayan ranges of thunder cloud, heavy and solemn with snow on their remote summits, turning yellow in the last light of evening, and both the ranges resounding with thunder as with reverberations of high mountain avalanches. At the western end of this valley in the sky, I followed the sun on its way down beyond the great mountain of Malabar. In my memory I saw it vividly retracing the route which I had been forced to follow into imprisonment—a route marked at all its critical phases for me by milestones of mountains, like the Goenoeng and Rajah Gedeh which stood over the Soekaboemi (the desired earth) where I had been thrown into my first "regular" prison with Nichols and his men; then on over the jungles of Bantam to another mountain, Djaja-Sempoer (the mountain of the arrow), which rose high over Lebaksembada (the valley that was well made), where I had my headquarters and below which I had walked into a Japanese trap; and finally on to Java Head and the Sunda Strait, out of whose coral waters rose the volcano of Krakatau.

I thought of all the times I had watched from the tip of the mountain-of-the-arrow, assailed by an immense feeling of doom, the great volcano's shattered rim wrapped in red-ragged sunsets and the dying light of day outlined beyond like a shadow of foreboding in a magic mirror of scarlet water, the tangled world of the vast island of Sumatra where I had begun my war in Southeast Asia. The feeling of doom was all the more disturbing then because it was not personal so much as cosmic almost, for I remember clearly how the end of the day then was always in my mind the end forever of an age of Empire and the night that came down swift as a bat, the fall of shadow implicit between end and re-beginning in the brief and brittle life of man.

It was odd, even to me, in spite of my own profound preoccupations, how that sunset evening seemed bent on a visual summing-up of my own journey towards and through imprisonment, almost as if it were some kind of end-of-term report. It was then that I saw in a crimson footprint of the sun a Bethlehem-bright star and the hair at the back of my shaven head suddenly went all a-tingle.

The hours that followed were even longer because, as the moment of lights-out approached that would give us darkness and quiet in which to try out the radio, my anxiety as to whether it would work grew with an almost unbearable intensity. In our over-crowded conditions, I could not take part in the listening operation myself, as I longed to do. Only one man at a time could do it and on this occasion in particular only an expert like the New Zealand officer who had made the radio could be that person.

I could picture him lying under his mosquito net with his ears pressed to the wooden clogs because at the best of times the sound which came out was as faint and difficult to follow as the sounds of radio I had first heard on a crystal set, as a boy in Africa some thirty years before. I could not possibly attempt to double-up with him under the net without giving the show away. I just had to compose myself as well as I could in the darkness under my net. I did not even have a watch with me to tell me what the time was or for that matter, that time had not stopped altogether as it felt to me.

I kept on wondering not only whether the set was working at all, but also, if it were working, which of the three stations we had contacted in the past was coming through. The listening officer had made three tiny coils which he slipped somewhere into his set to enable him to have a choice of three stations: if I remember rightly, Delhi in India, Perth in Australia, and San Francisco in America. On a good night, owing to the time differences of stations so far apart, we had managed in the past to get all three, but on this night I knew I would be profoundly grateful if he got only one.

I do not know how long I had been lying there in that state when I saw a movement against the sheen of the night at the open door. A dark shadow was outlined at the end of my mosquito net, and almost immediately afterwards I felt a hand tugging at my feet.

I crept out of my net as quietly as possible. Everybody else around me was fast asleep. I went out quietly to join the person who had touched me, in the shadows against the wall of our quarters. It was the New Zealand officer, who lost no time in whispering to me in a tone which carried much more than just the satisfaction and the excitement of success: "It worked, Colonel! It worked!"

By prearrangement, he said no more, because it was unsafe to talk at length in that situation, so near the guards and the entrance to the camp. We both walked across the quadrangle towards the long queue of men patiently waiting outside the latrines. Just out of earshot of the end of the queue he told me what had happened.

He had had some trouble making contact but after a great deal of fiddling had picked up a news broadcast from Delhi. Unfortunately he had not come in right at the beginning, but near enough it to realize that something tremendous had happened. He wasn't quite certain what precisely it was, but in the course of the morning of the day which was now ended, something more like an act of God than of man had been inflicted on Japan at a place called Hiroshima.

Exactly how and what had been done he couldn't tell. All he knew was that it was something new and terrible in human experience, more terrible even than earthquakes, tidal waves or volcanic eruptions. In fact he was not at all certain, when he recollected the emotion and excitement of the announcer's voice, whether it was news he had heard or not just an actor in some kind of horrific radio play.

But surely, I remarked, he could have told whether this was so or not from the rest of the news of how the war was going on elsewhere, which would normally have followed. That was precisely the trouble, he whispered, there was nothing but talk of this great kind of cataclysm which had taken place or had been inflicted on Japan, and speculation over its consequences, all of which it had been difficult to piece together and assess accurately, because the reception had not been all that good.

He was certain only that he had picked up an atmosphere of something which, if true, showed that the final turn of the tide in the war might have come. He assured me that, with some minor adjustments that he would make as a result of his listening in that night, he could verify all this in detail on all three of our usual stations twenty-four hours later.

At the end of all this I myself was in doubt whether we had a piece of real news or whether he had just got hold of some kind of dramatized radio fiction. I remembered how, before the war, a large section of the population of the United States had taken a radio dramatization of H. G. Wells's *The War of the Worlds* as a broadcast of real news and panicked. I wondered whether something similar had not happened at Delhi that night, and I was resolved, not that we should not panic, because there was no question of this, but that we should not jump to any premature conclusions.

On this note we dispersed, but I had only to catch a glimpse of the faces of Max al Kahdri and his friends the next morning to realize that they were in the grip of some tremendous excitement, and full of some kind of intimation of overwhelming portent. They looked as if they were on the point of bursting to tell me what it was, but, as I saw the men I knew to be spies as well as some others whom I suspected of the same role watching them closely, I gave them no encouragement and kept well away from them all day.

As far as the Japanese command was concerned however, I still could not detect the slightest trace of anything new in their attitudes. The silence and inactivity of the day before had vanished, the usual working parties were called for, and what was to us a normal day in those abnormal circumstances followed a routine course from roll call to lights-out, except that after another Götterdämmerung sunset just clearing the purple battlements of Malabar, there hung the bright sliver of the newest of new moons.

That night the New Zealand officer got through not only to Delhi but to Perth and San Francisco, and listened exclusively in to news and world comment and reactions which gave us a clear picture of what had happened at Hiroshima. Even now after all these years I, who know little about astrology, am not a follower of astrologers and who have no wish to make an astrological point of any kind at all, feel compelled to say that it looked at the very least most strange to me that the first atom bomb dropped by man should have been dropped on so moon-swung a people as the Japanese, during the phase of nothingness between the death of the oldest and the birth of the newest of new moons.

It is to me almost as if, out of the depths of life and time from the far fast expanding perimeter of our universe and its galaxies of star-foam, some cosmic impulse had come to extinguish the moon on this occasion so that its extinction and imminent rebirth could act on the limited awareness of man as an unmistakable symbol of annunciation that the past was dead and a new, greater phase of meaning about to reign on earth, however catastrophic the introduction.

I heard all this news of confirmation from the New
Zealand officer, of course, standing again at the end of
the latrine queue. We both had to follow the queue
through so as to establish that our presence there was
not a contrived pretense. I longed to break away and
get back to my own world under my mosquito net, to
come to terms with the news he had just told me and,
even more than coming to terms with it, try to interpret
and anticipate its consequences for us. But I dared not,
and to this day I do not know from where I got the
self-restraint to follow the slow, shuffling, tired file of
men through the latrines and out into the quadrangle
again, where the sky, heavy with stars, sagged lower
than ever on to the prison walls, and the dark was
brushed and illuminated from time to time as it were
by archangelic wings of lightning from the great
temple clouds sinking down into the rising tide of night
to vanish below the invisible horizon before morning
as they always did.

Ordering the New Zealand officer not to impart the
news to any other member of our group until I had
seen him in the morning, with a peremptoriness which
perhaps might have sounded unappreciative of the
near-miracle he had performed in getting us in radio
contact with the outside world again, I went to my
blanket on the stone floor.

I have remarked often enough how time stood still
for us in prison, because it was one of the most difficult
of all the conditions of imprisonment for us to accept,
and one with which we were in daily battle deep inside

ourselves; but from the moment I crept into my mosquito net, the whole nature of prison time became transformed. I found myself almost driven to the opposite extreme and complaining at the speed, the unbelievable acceleration with which it now surged forward. I did not sleep a wink, and yet it was the shortest night I have ever spent.

I seemed hardly to have crept under my net when through the phantom white mesh there was a glimmer of first light, and the hour had come for me to get up, shave and be ready for a new day. But in the lightning interval between going to bed and getting up, I had all the while in the pit of my stomach a warm feeling. I would say it was a warmth almost as if I had consumed a bottle of champagne, if I did not suspect this metaphor of being far too feeble to convey the unique lifegiving quality I was experiencing. Instinct alone suggests to me that it might well have been like the warmth experienced by a new-born child when feeling the first of its mother's milk starting up in its stomach the process of a life of its own.

For this is precisely how I finally interpreted the news. This cataclysm would end the war, and a new phase of life would inevitably result from it. This cataclysm I was certain would make the Japanese feel that they could now withdraw from the war without dishonour, because it would strike them, as it had us in the silence of our prison night, as something supernatural. They, too, could not help seeing it as an act of God more than an act of man, a Divine intimation that

STORY   : 101

they had to follow and to obey in all its implications.
The continuation of the war by what we, for want of a
better word and for fear of telling the truth, call "conventional means" would have left them locked in
the old, old situation of a battle of opposites in which
their whole history, culture and psychology would
have demanded death either in fighting or by their
own hand.

But this was something miraculously new, something not foreseen in their or our own philosophy. It
was something on so gigantic and undeniable a scale,
such a manifestation of new power at work in life, that
even they would know, as we who had been its terrible instrument of delivery would have to learn to
know, that all the old ways, laws, rules, conventions
and creeds which had brought us to this terrible im-
passe, had been judged invalid by life and something
else would have to take their place.

At last I was able to distinguish with confidence and
clarity between what was either wishful thinking or
fear of the future on one hand and valid intuition on
the other. The war with Japan was practically at an
end. Yet, as I was shaving, I was still aware that it was
a valid intuition under a shadow of suspicion which
warned me still to be on my guard so far as we ourselves were concerned. Although the war in general
appeared to be over, the issue for all of us in Southeast
Asia, my intuition seemed to warn, was not yet finally
decided in favour of life.

It was in this spirit that I told Nichols, and the of-

ficers in our confidence, of what had happened. I
begged them that we should not spread the news
wider but keep it strictly to ourselves until we knew
what its implications were to be for us. We had, I remember, a tremendous argument over this, in which I
stood alone for a time. Everyone thought that it would
be cruel not to spread the news immediately throughout the prison.

I thought the cruellest thing that could happen
would be to raise our prison mood into a state of eu-
phoria and then suddenly find it denied by events in
Southeast Asia, which were still under the command
of the inflexible Field-Marshal Terauchi, apparently as
impervious and independent as ever of the orders, let
alone the wishes, of his masters in Tokyo. I doubt
whether I would have won the argument if that very
day our Chinese contact had not suddenly sparked
into life and transmitted a brief but urgent warning
from Kim to be more on our guard than ever.

No explanations and no news of any kind accompanied the warning. It had obviously been most difficult to get through at all. Its epigrammatic form and
manner of delivery suggested clearly that it had been
transmitted not only under great difficulties, but in
conditions of extreme danger. I took Nichols aside and
told him for the first time of the course of my years of
lonely vigilance. Imaginative and far-seeing person
that he naturally was, he rallied to my side. Although
the camp was buzzing with rumours of all kinds like a

hive of bees about to swarm in the spring, we kept our counsel but, just as we had done in the past, without revealing any specific news we used the facts to guide rumour and speculation among our own men into what we felt were the safest and least harmful channels.

There was too, of course, another dread possibility to be considered. In a theater of war so far removed from Japan, the horror of Hiroshima could have the opposite effect of what my intuition and knowledge of the Japanese suggested to me it would have in Japan proper. The things human beings imagine are always so much worse than those they experience. Experience, however horrible, carries within itself its own built-in immunities for men but imagination, charged with the task of inventing a substitute for experience, always goes far beyond the realms of reality. Imagined injury and suffering I have always found, for instance, are far more difficult to come to terms with than suffering experienced and lived through to the end, no matter how terrible the suffering.

We had too to look at the truth of Hiroshima as we had done at all aspects of our conditions since the beginning of our captivity, not only steadily but whole, and to admit in the round that, once the news of the dropping of two atom bombs on Hiroshima and Nagasaki spread throughout Southeast Asia, down from Field-Marshal Terauchi to all his commanders and officers and men, a spirit of revenge, for what they would instinctively regard as a blasphemous outrage on their sacred land, would be added to the other motives they had for fighting to the end.

In particular, it could add fire to the many complicated inclinations towards revenge, on all the Europeans in their power, which I have already examined in detail. I think this aspect, more than any other of the arguments we had had among ourselves, convinced Nichols and the officers in the know that for the moment we had to be even more restrained and circumspect than ever before.

One significant sign was that the prison command themselves, from Korean guards and soldiers to the incorrigible and inexpressible Kasayama, the smouldering, volcanic Mori and their placid musical lieutenant, showed no indication whatever of being aware of what had happened in Japan.

I had from the moment I broke the news of Hiroshima and Nagasaki to Nichols also taken Jongejans fully into our confidence. Apart from knowing that there was no one in the camp I could trust more, I needed his own evaluation of the event to clarify and verify my own. We found ourselves in agreement. Moreover, even armed with all this certain knowledge as with a kind of microscope for scrutinizing the behavior of the Japanese with whom he was in daily contact, Jongejans at the end of every one of the few days which followed, reported to me that he could not observe any change in Japanese attitudes.

Clearly they had not been told because Terauchi

had not changed and this fact, added to this spark of a warning from the Chinese, suggested that somewhere high up in the Japanese chain of command the shock of Hiroshima and Nagasaki had registered in a way to give cause for alarm on our behalf.

I think it was not until five nights after we first had news of Hiroshima—the second bomb was dropped on Nagasaki three days later—that there was talk on the air of peace negotiations having been set in motion by the Emperor of Japan. The fact that the Emperor himself, this sacred personage who in the living mythology which motivated the imaginations and inspired the actions of the Japanese people was a descendant of the great Sun Goddess herself, had emerged into the vulgar glare of the news, seemed itself of the highest significance. Both Jongejans and I thought this confirmed our evaluation of the consequences of Hiroshima, and that it had indeed opened up for the Japanese a valid avenue of escape from the dilemma of a classical end to war. Only changes initiated and endorsed by the nearest human equivalent to a God of his people could succeed, in the circumstances, to relieve the fanatical military forces of their compulsion to fight to the last.

We had no idea at the time of how powerful these fanatical forces still were, despite their disastrous years of defeat and terrible retreat in the Pacific. We had no inkling then that the Emperor had only just succeeded in escaping suppression, if not assassination, at the hands of fanatical young service officers.

All I knew then was that, round about August 12th,

overtures for peace by the Emperor were openly discussed in the world; but I knew also that in our own theater of Southeast Asia there were rumours that Field-Marshal Terauchi was rejecting his own Emperor and refusing to follow him in his way to peace.

In fact I soon learned that Terauchi's stand had already so alarmed the Emperor and his advisors that he was sending his brother, Prince Chi-Chi-Bu, to Saigon to persuade the Field-Marshal to obey Tokyo and play his part in the general surrender that was about to take place.

Until the results of Prince Chi-Chi-Bu's mission to Terauchi were known, we had to accept the fact that we could not be sure of our own fate. How correct we were in this was again confirmed by the fact that from August 12th to I think August 17th I received more cryptic warnings, initiated presumably by Kim, that the danger to us was as great as ever.

By this time rumours, and an interchange of euphoric interpretations of what had happened in the world outside, were poured into the ears of our men by their Dutch, Ambonese, Menadonese and Chinese fellow-prisoners. Everyone was seething with excitement, with belief that the war was at an end. There was wild talk among the Dutch of breaking out of the camp if they were not released soon. I had to plead desperately with the Dutch command to restrain the rumours, and to deny over-optimistic interpretations of events for a while, because unless we kept to the

routine of behaviour that we had followed up to now
we might provide the Japanese command with precisely the sort of excuse for which their minds might
be groping in order to justify their taking revenge on
us.

Yet I knew that it could only be a matter of days if
not hours now before all the dammed-up emotions of
three and a half years in prison would burst through
the walls of restraint, and overwhelm not only the
Dutch but perhaps our own men, and particularly my
own small group of beloved Australians, compelling
them to acts which could have terrible repercussions
for us all. I was so much aware of this that I fully accepted the fact that within a day or two, even if there
were no clarification of Field-Marshal Terauchi's attitude, we would have to take all our officers and men
fully into our confidence at whatever the risks of ex-
posure to our own prison command. We would then
have to explain to them and reason at length why they
should continue in what would seem to them such un-
natural and unnecessary restraint. I feared we would
explain and reason without success, even so.

From the night of August 17th, when I think we first
heard of the final Japanese capitulation, the tension
for me, charged to provide for our own special fate,
was as great as ever and I was in a state of perpetual
argument with myself because, not only did the Japanese in charge of our camp continue to behave as if
they had not yet heard even of Hiroshima, let alone

peace negotiations and capitulation, but there was still no news of the outcome of Prince Chi-Chi-Bu's mission to Saigon.

All this time we had our daily parades and roll calls at first light and sunset as usual. They were conducted by Gunzo Mori and his guards in the same arrogant manner as before. Closely as one looked for signs of change in them, neither Jongejans nor I could yet discern even the faintest hint of a difference. If anything, their confidence and rigidity of rule seemed greater than before. The only indication that somewhere high up there might have been a sign of change to come was the fact that suddenly no more working parties were called for. All of us were confined to our camp all day long. No traders were allowed at the gates and we were sealed off from the outside world more effectively than ever before. This last, combined with the absence of change in the attitude of the prison command to us, suggested that as far as we were concerned the issue between life and death might not yet have been decided. It all continued still to look pretty ominous to me.

From August 17th to August 21st, technically a period of only four days, time did not stand still for me even, but at moments appeared to be caught up in a violent stage of regression in the mind of the Japanese command far back towards some terrible archaic moment in the evolution of their national spirit. How little the Japanese had changed seemed to me to come to a focus in something reported to me by one of our officers after the morning parade on August 21st. He was a Royal Air Force officer called Ian Horobin, now Sir Ian Horobin and an ex-minister of the British Crown.

Horobin was one of the men in Nichols's first group. Moreover he was a person to whom I owed my own life. From his work at staff headquarters before the Allied capitulation in 1942, he knew of my secret mission in the jungles of west Java and the whereabouts of my base in Bantam. He had been caught by the Japanese on his way to join me. Although beaten and tortured for information he had not succumbed and given me away. He was one of the few officers with whom we had regularly shared our news, and, of course, he had been told of the final Japanese capitulation. He was a deeply religious person, and in the various prisons where we had been at times without priests he had conducted services for us and delivered some remarkable sermons, of great intelligence and originality, uplifted with a touch of the poet that he was. He had in fact written in prison a most moving poem about a particularly brutal execution that we had been made to witness early on—a poem called "Java Sunday," since the execution had taken place on a Sunday afternoon, one of the most beautiful I have ever seen, to sharpen the ugliest of deeds.

On this particular morning Horobin told me that he and five other officers had joined the official Royal Air Force chaplain, Squadron-Leader Giles, at dawn, as they often did for receiving the sacrament. The place

where "Padre" Giles always performed this service
was in a far corner of the camp. Nearby there were
two massive wooden gates which had been heavily
boarded and shored up by the Japanese for obvious
reasons. It was, although Horobin did not know it, intended to be one of the main targets of our attack
should the Japanese try to massacre us—one of the
four points in prison through which we intended during the confusion of the fighting to slip one of the four
men we had selected as our messengers.

There was one crack in the heavy wood of the gates
through which one could see something of the world
outside, if one were brave enough to risk detection by
the guards; a Menadonese who tried it once had been
beaten senseless and was afterwards sentenced to a
week's solitary confinement.

Just before their service of Holy Communion, Horobin said, he had dared to peer through the crack. In
the light of an immense and fast spreading red dawn,
he had seen the Japanese soldiers responsible for
guarding the camp go on parade. The parade, he said,
was like all the other parades one had witnessed in
ampler days of confinement. It had ended as usual
with all the soldiers bowing their heads reverently in
the direction of the rising sun.

Horobin told me that not only did the soldiers look
so totally unaware of Hiroshima and Nagasaki and the
abject defeat of their country, but also so completely
without any intimation of what might await them
after surrender, from their trial as war criminals to
which we knew from our radio the Allies were irre-

vocably determined to subject them, that, quite unbidden, such a rush of pity and compassion surged in
him that he found himself in tears for them.

Horobin's story moved me more than I can say because it was for me the final evidence that the way
they had all lived through three and a half years of
prison had turned defeat into such a victory that not
even death by massacre, should it come, could rob
them of it.

Then, early in the afternoon after a long hot morning, I was suddenly sent for by the Japanese. This was
so unusual, because I was not the senior British officer,
that it alarmed me. I had never been sent for in this
way before, and I had to face the possibility that it
could be a singularly bad omen. It could mean, for
example, that my contacts had been discovered and
had been made to talk, and that the talk would lead
the Japanese to the worst possible conclusions regarding me, because of the cloud of suspicion under which
I had initially been released into Nichols's first camp.

It could be the prelude to the end of which I had
been so consistently warned. For the moment a small
still voice, deep within me, suggesting that the Japanese might perhaps be sending for me for the best possible reasons, was utterly silenced. I had time only to
tell my own secret second-in-command that if I were
not back within a few hours he should report to
Nichols and the Dutch sapper colonel, and prepare for
the kind of final battle within the prison walls for
which we had so long planned.

I was conducted by the indefatigable Kasayama to

the Japanese commander's office. Neither he nor Gunzo Mori were there, but a new Japanese sergeant-major, whom I had never seen before, with a staff-band round his arm, was waiting for me. He immediately led me out of the office and into a large car waiting, a Japanese soldier at the wheel. We were driven off quickly to a broad villa in *Lembang*. This hamlet, at the foot of Tangkoeboehan-praauw, was the place where General Wavel once had his combined headquarters and where he himself had given me the secret orders for the mission which was to lead to my capture. The villa itself had belonged before the war to a Dutch oil tycoon. It had large, luxurious grounds and a wide gravelled drive leading up to a broad verandah. The grounds were full of staff cars, with military chauffeurs standing at the ready beside them.

At the sight a great surge of hope almost unmanned me. I suddenly became conscious of my own incongruous appearance. I was bare-legged and wore a pair of prison-made wooden clogs. I had on a pair of khaki shorts, nearly rotted through by the sun and kept together only by constant patching and repairing. I had on a khaki shirt in a similar condition and crude prison-made badges of rank, sewn awkwardly on to the shoulder straps of my shirt. I had lost my military hat in captivity, and wore instead a khaki cap which had been made for me by an Australian officer who had been a dress designer in civilian life. The peak of the hat had been stiffened by cardboard and I had to be careful not to wear it when it rained because the sodden cardboard would sag and the peak fall over my eyes. Fortunately the afternoon was still hot and dry.

My Australian soldiers had also, in a manner which touched me deeply, made their own idea of an appropriate military badge for my hat. Because they knew I had been born in Africa, it was not a copy of the badge of the British regiment in which I had been commissioned, but the head in miniature of what they took to be the African antelope, which the South African soldiers they had known in the Western desert wore. The metal out of which they had made it came from a fragment of a Japanese plane shot down before the capitulation, and somehow left lying in one of our camps. They had not been very expert in the making of the hat. Not only was it not symmetrical but in the course of a clash with a Japanese guard one day, one of the horns of the badge had been permanently crumpled. I could not have looked more of a caricature of an officer.

However, I followed the orderly up the steps and through the door with as much dignity as I could muster from within my confused and bewildered self, and with as much firmness as my depleted physique allowed. The large room into which I was ushered seemed full of senior staff officers. When they all rose as I entered and bowed to me, I knew beyond the last limit of doubt that I had been summoned for the best of all possible reasons.

Something in me indeed must have anticipated this already, because I made no attempt to remove my hat. In normal prison circumstances this would have been one of the most provocative things I could have done. As the full meaning of this immense and punctiliously polite Japanese welcome came to me, relief, emotion and a thousand and one urgent and complex feelings made me weak at the knees and I began to tremble violently within; yet I managed to acknowledge their bows with a firm but perfunctory salute.

I was politely asked to sit down in a leather arm-chair but refused and stood there silent, keeping upright only with an immense effort, which I hoped was not noticeable, while some decanters of wine and wine glasses appeared. The glasses were filled all round and a glass of wine offered first to me. I declined it.

Then the general and his officers all raised their glasses and the general himself, who I was to discover afterwards had been on military secondment to England, held out his glass to me and said: "I drink sincerely to your victory." They all emptied their glasses in one draught and as I still stood there silent, hoping I was not looking quite as near collapse as I felt, the general spoke again. I heard him, not like someone in the room with me so much as like a voice speaking into my ear through the receiver at the end of a long trunkline of time and history: "We Japanese have decided to switch, and when we Japanese switch, we switch sincerely."

I need not here go into the reasons why I had been

sent for. It had nothing to do with life in prison but with issues graver even than the question of our own survival had been, and part of another story which must be told elsewhere. All that matters here is that when I ultimately got back to camp, after giving the Japanese a series of precise orders, I reached our old prison to find it in a state of intense activity. The senior officers in command had been politely requested, and for the first time in our prison history not ordered, to muster all the men, for departure by train that very night to the great port and city of Batavia as it was then called.

Soon after dark, some thousands of men and hundreds of their fellows too weak to walk, many nearly dying and carried on stretchers, marched out of the prison for the last time, all of them on the first stage of their way to liberation and home; except me myself, who was now faced with another immediate mission, physically weak as I was, and with several more years of a new sort of war in Southeast Asia ahead of me. But the feeling of gratitude to life and Providence that all these men were safe at last overwhelmed everything else in me at that moment. It was a feeling as of music everywhere within and about me.

As I watched the long slow procession of men march into the night, this feeling of music everywhere rose within my liberated senses like a chorale at the end of a great symphony, asserting a triumph of creation over death. All that was good and true in the dark experience behind me, combined with my memory of how those thousands of men, who had endured so much, never once had failed to respond to the worst with what was best in them, and all that had happened to me, in some mysterious fashion seemed to have found again the abiding rhythm of the universe, and to be making such a harmony of the moment as I have never experienced.

All I was feeling then, so utterly beyond words, seemed confirmed when I looked up and saw that the clear receptive air, standing so still and high like the water of a deep well in that raised plain of Bandoeng, was beginning to fill with the light of a rising moon. *That* moon which symbolizes so much of the spirit of unfailing renewal, not only of the Japanese but of all men and all living things, was itself full and overflowing. It seemed suddenly to send, unbidden, another great light over the rim of my war-darkened memory, flooding my heart with a bright feeling of continuity, restoring me to the stream of all the life that had ever been and ever could be. The feeling quickly transformed itself into the most evocative of words. The words were not my own but those of one of a moving D. H. Lawrence poem, a declaration of the rights of life, based on the image of the moon, beginning with the bugle call:

> And who has seen the moon, who has not seen
> Her rise from out the chamber of the deep,
> Flushed and grand and naked . . .

The poem ascended from there on in my mind in great

chords of music to the final affirmation that when the moon is "spread out and known at last"

> ... We are sure
> That beauty is a thing beyond the grave,
> That perfect, bright experience never falls
> To nothingness, and time will dim the moon
> Sooner than our full consummation here
> In this odd life will tarnish or pass away.

I thought instantly then that the poem had come to me at that moment because alone on a Japanese tramp steamer, barely nineteen and on my way back from Japan to Africa in 1926, I had first read this poem on a moonlit sea off Java, and had been inexpressibly touched by it. I realized however, a second later, it had done so even more because it introduces a series of poems that make up one of the greatest and most uncompromising manifestoes of life written in my generation under the title: "Look! We have come through!"

"A REMARKABLE THOUGHT"

Men think by fits and starts.
And if they think, they fasten
Their hands upon their hearts.

A. E. HOUSMAN

I TRIED TO COMPRESS the quintessence of all this into the ten minutes I had with the shrivelled little Japanese doctor in the television studio in America that evening. I tried to stress how certain I was that if the atom bombs had not been dropped on Hiroshima and Nagasaki, the war would have dragged on, the Japanese would have fought as they had fought everywhere else to the bitter end, from island to island, and so on to the last, in the islands of Japan proper. I told him that I believed this because those two terrible bombs must have seemed as supernatural to the Japanese as they had seemed to me when I first heard of them in the darkness and the danger of our own prison. Somewhere in the unconscious minds of the Japanese people, I argued with the eloquence of an absolute conviction, it must have looked as if their Sun Goddess Ama-Terasu herself had hurled fragments of her sun at Japan to shatter it out of its suicidal course and show it in incontrovertible fashion that it had to stop and mend its ways. After all, had not they themselves described the flash which preceded the first mushroom cloud at Hiroshima: "Brighter than a thousand suns"?

I told him how certain I was that the Emperor could never have gathered round himself sufficient influen-

tial voices to make the party of peace win the day, and
that he himself might have been assassinated, as he
very nearly was, by some of the more fanatical and
younger Japanese officers. The war would have
dragged on and apart from many many more Japanese
dead, hundreds and thousands of Americans and their
allies would have died as well. Above all for me, selfish
as it may sound, there was the certain knowledge that
if the bomb had not been dropped and the Emperor
had not been able to intervene, Field-Marshal Terauchi would have fought on and the prisoners in his
power would have been killed. I made clear to him
that, although I had done no definite research into the
matter and had no accurate statistics available, I had
heard enough from prisoners-of-war in other areas of
Field-Marshal Terauchi's command to estimate that
anything between 200,000 and 400,000 people would
have been massacred. Even had we not been deliberately massacred, we were near our physical end
through lack of food. The war had only to drag on
some months longer for most of us to have perished.
But quite apart from the death through starvation
which threatened us there was, most important for me,
this question of a deliberate massacre.

The date for this was to be co-ordinated with the
day on which the Allied invasion began in the Southeast Asian theater of war that was under Terauchi's
command. We knew now that this invasion, by forces
under command of Lord Mountbatten, was planned
and ready to begin on September 6th, that is to say,

within three weeks of the Japanese capitulation. As far as the many hundreds of thousands of prisoners and internees in Southeast Asia were concerned therefore, death by all counts had been a near miss. There would have been no miss at all if it had not been for Hiroshima and Nagasaki, and I would not be there to speak to him.

I admitted that he could, perhaps, still suspect this part of my reasoning. I could imagine that he might accept more readily an hypothesis that if the war had gone on longer the military casualties would have been many hundreds of thousands greater and that, as far as we in prison were concerned, whether we would have lived or not was purely conjecture, and death by deliberate killing far from a certainty. Indeed he may well have thought that all I had told him about myself and my fellow-prisoners in Java was just part of a natural fear created by the strains of years of imprisonment. In that connection, I hoped he would believe me, when I told him that, when I went back to active service and joined the staff of Lord Mountbatten, I discussed this aspect of our imprisonment fully with Lord Mountbatten's Director of Military Intelligence, an experienced officer called General Penney, whom I had known well. He had been my tutor at a staff-college and I had worked closely with him on an urgent mission on which he and I were sent by Lord Mountbatten to the War Cabinet in London.

General Penney had assured me that, among the staff records captured at Terauchi's headquarters, evidence was found of plans to kill all prisoners and internees when the invasion of Southeast Asia began in earnest. I begged the doctor, therefore, to accept that, terrible as the dropping of the two atom bombs had been, his wife and the many thousands who died with her had died in order to save the lives of many hundreds of thousands more. I had tried to speak to him in this way not only for myself but for thousands thus saved, and would like him to know how we would be forever in his wife's debt as well as that of her fellow-victims.

Those of us who had survived like him and myself could only discharge our debt by looking as deeply and as honestly as we could into the various contributions we had made to this disaster. The war and the bomb, after all, had started in ourselves before they struck in the world without, and we had to look as never before into our small individual lives and the context of our various nations. We who were saved seemed to me charged by life itself to live in such a way now that no atom bomb could ever be dropped again, and war need never again be called in, as it had been throughout recorded history, as the terrible healer of one-sidedness and loss of soul in man. Could I through him thus presume to acknowledge my debt of life to his wife and beg him to believe she had not died in vain?

Whether I had helped him by my story, and whether he agreed with my conclusions, I could not tell for certain. All I know is that at the end of our television discussion, before we left on our separate ways, he bowed to me as the Japanese general and his officers on that fateful August day had done.

Hissing between his teeth as the old-fashioned Japanese used to do when moved, he came out of his bow to say: "Would you please be so kind as to allow me to thank you for a remarkable thought."

He added to that, after a pause, the traditional farewell of the Japanese, which in itself reflects much of their spirit charged so heavily with provision of fate: the Sayonara that just means: "If it must be."

Postscript

T HE QUESTION MAY well be asked why this story was not told twenty-five years ago. There are two main answers to the question. One is that when I came out of prison in August 1945, I went straight back to active service without even a day's leave. For close on the eighteen months that followed I was involved in another kind of war, both military and political, in Indonesia. Militarily, it was a desultory and minor war compared with the war which had preceded it but for me, at any rate, it was often as dangerous and always more unpleasant because, among other things, unlike its predecessor, its objectives were confused and dubious.

When the British forces could at last be withdrawn from Indonesia towards the end of 1946, I was ordered to stay on as Military Attaché to the British minister in Java. I could not return to Britain until a year later, like some kind of military Rip Van Winkle, so quickly and completely forgotten was the decade of war, imprisonment and more war to which I belonged. I immediately found myself confronted on my return with another special challenge as personal and, to me, even more important and urgent than the one which had made me go straight from prison to active service.

This challenge constituted the second reason that made it impossible for me to give my mind to the theme of this story.

It all arose out of the fact that the most disturbing feature for me of all the years I had spent in Indonesia which I had come to love with almost as great an intensity as my native Africa, was the discovery that a people so intelligent, admirable and efficient as the Dutch, unbelievable as it may now seem, had managed to live in Indonesia for some 350 years without apparently ever suspecting even that in the secret hearts of the millions of people they governed, well after a Roman fashion, the greatest desire from the beginning had been to be quit of them and their rule. This aspect of life in Indonesia, this kind of insensitivity of Empire, seemed to me the outstanding example of the cause of all the great and growing European trouble in the Far East.

But far more important and immediate to me, was the realization it spread within my own heart that in my native continent of Africa, as I looked back to it under the microscope of the intensest nostalgia which only imprisonment and living daily with a threat of death can produce, this same form of unawareness among its European rulers was even greater than it had ever been in Indonesia. I had, ever since I can remember, been opposed to colour prejudice in my own country. I had written, when barely more than a boy, one of the first books on the evil of colour and race prejudices and so was quick to feel as a result of my time in Java that, unless something were done to make the European in British Africa and particularly in my own native South Africa aware of the evils and perils implicit in a similar lack of imagination and insensitivity to the inner needs and desires of the peoples of Africa, even greater disasters faced them there than those they were already experiencing in Asia.

Accordingly, the moment I was free of the special sense of obligation which had made me serve on in Java I felt compelled to do what I could in my own small way to set this right. In spite of tempting offers of promotion and a career of interest in an army for which I had acquired a profound admiration and affection, I resigned from it. I devoted years that followed to work in Africa, trying to help prevent a repetition of the amply discredited patterns of history which dominate so large a part of the great continent today.

All this meant that I had neither the freedom of imagination nor the time to give to the aspect of my experience with which this story is concerned. But I doubt whether, even if I had had the time and the mind, I would have written the story as I have written it here much before today. I believe I would have decided against it because, even told as I believe I would have told it at the moment of Japan's surrender, without resentment against the Japanese, I would have been afraid that it would have been used just as more atrocity evidence for the punishment which was being inflicted on our enemies for the war and the manner in which they had conducted it.

I myself was utterly opposed to any form of war trials. I refused to collaborate with the officers of the various war crimes tribunals that were set up in the Far East. There seemed to me something unreal, if not utterly false, about a process that made men, like war crimes investigators from Europe, who had not suffered under the Japanese more bitter and vengeful about our suffering than we were ourselves. There seemed in this the seeds of the great, classic and fateful evasions in the human spirit which, I believe, both in the collective and in the individual sense, have been responsible for most of the major tragedies of recorded life and time and are increasingly so in the tragedies that confront us in the world today. I refer to the tendencies in men to blame their own misfortunes and those of their cultures on others; to exercise judgement they need for themselves in the lives of others; to search for a villain to explain everything that goes wrong on their private and collective courses. It was easy to be high-minded always in the life of others and afterwards to feel one had been high-minded in one's own. The whole of history, it seemed to me, had been bedevilled by this unconscious and instant mechanism of duplicity in the mind of man. As I saw it, we had no moral surplus in our own lives for the lives of others. We needed all our moral energies for ourselves and our own societies.

I had been drawn steadily over the years to a conclusion which has become almost a major article of faith. Men, I believed, were their own greatest villain —they themselves the flies in their own ointment. Villains undoubtedly do exist in the wide world without. But they do so in a mysterious and significant state of inter-dependence with the profoundest failures and inadequacies in ourselves and our attitudes to life. It is almost as if the villain without is a Siamese twin of all that is wrong within ourselves. The only sure way to rid life of villains, I believed, after years of thinking about it in prison, was to rid ourselves first of the villain within our own individual and native collective contexts. If we could take care of the measure of the failures in ourselves, I was certain that the world on the whole would ultimately take better care of itself.

I felt strongly that if war had had any justification at all it was only in the sense that at its end, it should leave victors and vanquished free for a moment from the destructive aspects of their past. Modern war appeared to me a grim autonomous state of life carrying within itself, its own harsh system of reward and punishment for those who waged it. It was almost as if war today were a bitter form of penance for all our inadequate yesterdays. Once this terrible penance had been paid, my own experience suggested, it re-established men in a brief state of innocence which, if seized with imagination, could enable us to build better than before. To go looking for particular persons and societies to blame and punish at the end of war seemed to me to throw men back into the negative aspects of the past from which they had been trying to escape, and to deprive them of the opportunity they had so bitterly earned to begin afresh.

In any case, I did not believe then as I do not believe now, that you could punish whole peoples or even solitary individuals into being better persons. This seemed a renegade, discredited and utterly archaic concept. It has been tried throughout history. Far from being an instrument of redemption, which is punishment's only moral justification, it is an increasingly self-defeating weapon in the hands of dangerously one-sided men. I know only that I came out of prison longing passionately—and I am certain my longing was shared by all the thousands of men who had been with me—that the past would be recognized as the past and instantly buried before it spread another form of putrefaction in the spirit of our time. I thought that the only hope for the future lay in an all-embracing attitude of forgiveness of the peoples who had been our enemies. Forgiveness, my prison experience had taught me, was not mere religious sentimentality; it was as fundamental a law of the human spirit as the law of gravity. If one broke the law of gravity one broke one's neck; if one broke this law of forgiveness one inflicted a mortal wound on one's spirit and became once again a member of the chain-gang of mere cause and effect from which life has labored so long and painfully to escape.

The conduct of thousands of men in war and in prison with me confirmed with an eloquence which is one of my most precious memories of war, that the spirit of man is naturally a forgiving spirit. I was convinced that if the cancellation of the negative past which is forgiveness could take its place, it would automatically be followed by the recognition that men could no longer change the pattern of life for the better by changing their frontiers, their systems and their laws of compulsion of judgement and justice, but only by changing themselves.

I had learnt to fear the Pharisee more than the sinner; judgement and justice almost more than human error. I know judgement and justice had brought us far but that *far* was not far enough. Only the exercise of the law of forgiveness, the declaration forever of an unconditional amnesty for all in the warring spirit of men, could carry us on beyond. This alone could be the beginning of real change in life and it could only be by example of patiently living out the change in ourselves that we could hope to change for the better the societies to which we belong. It had become axiomatic for me that we could take nobody and no people further than we had taken ourselves. To the extent to which I felt my own war experience could contribute to such a shift in the imagination of man, I responded as a matter of inner urgency—despite all the other preoccupations that beset me—and very soon after my return from Java, put it as well as I could into a story called "A Bar of Shadow"—a theme I later orchestrated in a longer book called *The Seed and the Sower*. However, as far as the day-to-day facts of what we had endured under the Japanese were concerned, I preferred to remain silent, because I was convinced that the use to which they inevitably would be put in this literal and two-dimensionally minded age of ours, would work against the whole truth of war and the meaning and consequences it should have for the world.

I would have remained silent even now if it had not been for the fact that I see another kind of one-sidedness being introduced into the thinking of our time, as dangerous as the other one-sidedness that I feared in ourselves at the end of the war. This one-sidedness results from the fact that more and more people see the horror of Hiroshima and Nagasaki out of context. They tend to see it increasingly as an act of history in which we alone were the villains. I have been amazed to observe how in some extraordinary kind of way my own Japanese friends do not seem to feel that they had done anything themselves to provoke us into inflicting Hiroshima and Nagasaki on them and how strangely uncurious they are about their own part in the war. I felt that it was extremely important for them as well as for us to maintain a view of this cataclysmic event as steady as it was whole. I had a feeling almost as if I had been placed in a special position by life to contribute in a small way to what should be the final wholeness of the concept of the history of that moment. Perhaps no particular event in history is fully accounted for until it has been seen also from the point of view of the persons who had a special relationship with it. It is precisely because I am convinced that the thousands of people who were in prison with me, and I in particular, had a special relationship with this terrible moment in time that I felt I had a duty to put my share of it on record.

This sense of duty has become more acute as the time left for me to do so has become less. There was too the obvious danger that something essential of the experience would be forgotten. The statistics of what happened to us were perhaps not imperilled. But what seemed to me to be increasingly in danger were the great imponderables of those years that conceived our experience, gave it its own unique life and clothed the bare bones of facts and statistics of our existence with something precious and irrevocable of our perishable flesh and blood.

A NOTE ON THE
BACKGROUND
OF THE STORY

NICHOLS AND I, who had come with our men to the Bandoeng prison from confinement in far grimmer circumstances at a place called Soekaboemi—the name for us always was profoundly ironical because it means "The desired earth"—were to look back on our first term in Bandoeng as the "golden age" of our captivity. The Japanese, surprised by the speed and extent of their conquests in Southeast Asia, had not yet had time to develop a definite prisoner-of-war policy, nor to create a special prisoner-of-war administration. We were, to start with, at the haphazard mercies of the Japanese fighting forces and brutal as their treatment of us could be, they were better than the special prison administration which was set up later, run as it was by inferior officers and warrant officers in command of fanatical Korean guards. We suffered on the whole under the Koreans more than we had done at the hands of regular Japanese troops.

Above all, the Japanese army, whose business was war, quite apart from despising us for having allowed ourselves to fall into their hands alive, took only a spasmodic interest in us. Between "blitzes," as we called their periodic outbursts against us, there were long periods in which we were left comparatively free to regulate our own affairs within the walls of our prison. Had it not been for those casual months at Bandoeng, I do not believe we would have come out of prison either as well as we did or for that matter alive. Those months of comparative neglect, in the military sense, gave Nichols and me time to organize ourselves in the manner I have described in the main story.

It enabled me, for instance, to develop a system of contact with my Chinese friends outside, who just on my spoken word that the British Government would pay them back after the war, lent me vast sums of money to supplement our criminally inadequate diet. We both knew that our Bandoeng fortunes could not last and that by far our best investment was in proteins and cereals, to make our men as fit as possible for what we knew were long lean years ahead. But we both knew too that men, particularly the men from the British Commonwealth that we had with us, could not live by rice alone and that they had other kinds of hunger as much in need of satisfying.

We created accordingly a vast prison organization for the re-education of ourselves, a sort of prison kindergarten, school, high school, technical college and university rolled into one. At one end of the scale we had a British officer, Major Pat Lancaster of the Fourth Hussars, teaching a couple of splendid Australians from the Never-Never of their country to read and write. At the other end was "Don" Gregory—a don from Oxbridge but committed to war as an erk in the Royal Air Force—coaching people for their bachelor and master of arts degrees. We had an active school of drama, as active a school of music and an extensive faculty of arts and crafts. The whole of this side of our life in prison was one of my special responsibilities, since Nichols, as the senior British officer, had his hands over-full already in dealing with the administration of the camp and, above all, the exacting Japanese. But the person on whom this, for us, vast and creative prison edifice was well and truly founded was a remarkable scholar of French, a sensitive Welshman of great quality and imagination, called Gunner Rees, M.A. Nichols and I gave him the prison title of Director of Education, and I can only say that I wish he were Director of Education in Britain today.

The arts and crafts faculty of this university, which attracted almost as many Dutch, Menadonese, Ambonese and Chinese prisoners to it as British, was very dear to Rees and it owed a great deal to him. At the same time he helped me more than I can say to make our prison schoolmasters, professors and artists aware of the fact that one of their main functions was to keep alive in our men their sense of continuity. The greatest psychological danger threatening men in the conditions of imprisonment we had to endure was the feeling that imprisonment was a complete break with their past and totally unconnected with their future lives. This danger we overcame in such a triumphant manner that, with exceptions which I could count on the fingers of one hand, imprisonment for our men was transformed from an arid waste of time and life into one of the most meaningful experiences they had ever known.

In order to encourage in particular this vital sense of continuity in our prison camp, our arts and crafts faculty was charged with the duty of collecting material for making a memorial book, which we intended to publish at the end of our imprisonment. Dutch, English and Australian artists were encouraged to draw and paint anything which they thought memorable, for illustration in the book.

A portrait of Wing-Commander W. T. H. Nichols was done by Sid Scales, a New Zealand officer in the Royal Air Force and a Catalina reconnaissance pilot in Southeast Asia. He was an unusually gifted draftsman with a particular aptitude for caricature. This portrait of Nichols was one of a series of cartoons he did for us under the heading of "Campicatures."

Portraits of Cicurel and Donaldson were done by a Dutch artist, a private in the Dutch Colonial army, called Kees van Willingen, who was a member of our prison faculty and a person to whom we owed much. Van Willingen and Scales between them did portraits of everybody who was of any interest and meaning to our life in camp, with the exception of myself. In fact I am the only senior officer of our Bandoeng group who was not drawn.

As the officer responsible for all this side of our life in camp, despite all their urging, I refused to have my own portrait done. I had no rational reason but only an instinctive motive for my refusal—a feeling that the more "nonpersonal" I was about my rôle in camp, the better I would be able to perform it. Looking back, it seems to me, I feared that having my portrait done would be putting myself and what I was trying to do in a more egotistical dimension than the one in which I saw my rôle. There is therefore no contemporary portrait of myself available, and the nearest I can get to this period in time is a photograph of myself taken some two years after the war, when I was on my way back from my post as Military Attaché to the British minister in Java, to report to the War Office and the British Government in London.

Although in the story I have called it "Al Kahdri's secret radio," he was not the chief person concerned with it. The inspiration of the group of gallant young officers who made this radio and ran it so successfully in camp came, if I remember rightly, from a young Dutch fighter pilot who had been shot down in an air battle over Malaya and had been badly burned. I regret that I cannot remember his name and give him personal credit for what his group accomplished.

This radio set, unlike ours, was built into two Dutch military water flasks cut vertically down the center and hinged at the bottom. In the daytime the earphones were dismantled, removed and safely hidden away in the camp so that if they were discovered they would have looked like some sort of scrap left behind by the Dutch before capitulation. The top halves of the flasks were then clamped back into their normal position and restored to their canvas containers.

We ourselves in evolving our own secret radio had gone through this phase and built a radio in field flasks, but had quickly abandoned the method when I learned from a secret source that a Dutch working party on its way out from Java had been searched before boarding their ship. A radio was found in their field flasks and both the owners of the flasks and the officer in charge had been decapitated for what the Japanese regarded as one of the most serious crimes of which a prisoner could be culpable.

I believe that Max al Kahdri and his group were extremely lucky to have escaped detection, particularly in view of the close watch kept on them by the spies I mention in my story. To this day I am certain that if our imprisonment had continued only a few weeks longer, they too would have been discovered and undergone a similar punishment.

A newspaper called *Mark Time* was also part of our strategy for quickening the feeling of continuity in the minds of our men which I have mentioned, as well as a stimulated sense of belonging, and an awareness of both knowing and being known. It was too our best means of keeping at bay the rumour-mongering which had such destructive effects among the Dutch and to which I refer in the story.

In it we published daily translations of the news from the official Japanese newspapers and such journals in Malay as we could obtain. We translated this news in a way which would have appeared faithful to foreigners but to anyone whose language was English would have had quite another content. This content, without our saying so to the camp in general, came from our knowledge of the real news obtained on our secret radio. Knowing the real news enabled us to direct our readers so that they could interpret the Japanese and Malay reports about the progress of the war more truthfully.

With the news went reports on the daily life of the men at their work and of events in the camp. There were also illustrated magazine supplements filled with short stories, feature articles, poems and essays about the world without and the life from which our men from all over the Commonwealth had come. As the supplies of paper left behind by the Dutch were consumed, all our writings were increasingly produced on Japanese lavatory paper.

I regret that I do not remember the name of the first editor of *Mark Time*. He was with us only for a very short while and was not one of my or Nichols's group, but I remember him well as a person—a Yorkshireman and a gunner—a young man of character with a voice that seemed to ring straight out of Shakespeare's England. When he left us with the first working party to be sent away from Java, the editorship was taken over by an Australian officer, Pilot-Officer Webb, a professional journalist. Webb from the start ran *Mark Time* superbly, with the help of a Royal Air Force corporal, now Group-Captain, Michael Dyer, who had a lively gift for writing. When Dyer too left us in a working party for Japan, Webb carried on *Mark Time* brilliantly with various helpers until its "untimely" end.

We called the paper *Mark Time* because of a joke I made at the first meeting I had with the men who helped me to organize all these activities in the camp. Someone at this meeting had remarked how in Java there were apparently no seasons and how not only life in prison but nature itself seemed to stand still. I had commented: "Yes, time in Java reminds me very much of Lloyd George's description of Ramsay Mac-Donald's behaviour as a statesman. Lloyd George, in the British House of Commons, rebuked MacDonald one day with the remark that 'the honourable member for Lossiemouth—Ramsay MacDonald—reminds me of nothing more than a person marking time with suffi-cient agility to give the appearance of a man moving forward.'" There was a laugh and the Yorkshire gun-ner suggested instantly that we should borrow from Lloyd George and call our paper *Mark Time*.

The artist, Ray Parkin, whose drawing of a Japanese sword appears in this volume, was one of the founder members of our arts and crafts faculty at Bandoeng. He was a professional sailor and a warrant officer in the Royal Australian Navy and one of the survivors of the Australian cruiser *Perth* which, in the company of an American cruiser *Houston* and a small Dutch de-stroyer *Evertzen*, took on the whole of the formidable Japanese invasion fleet in the Sunda Strait on the night of March 1, 1942. This tiny force, crippled already by heavy action against superior Japanese naval forces in the battle of the Java Sea, and with its supplies of ammunition low, fought one of the most heroic naval engagements on record.

Ray Parkin, a quartermaster of the *Perth*, steered the ship throughout the action. He was in fact the last man to abandon the cruiser and did so only when his captain, "Hooky" Bell, who went down with the ship, ordered him "to get the hell out of it." All this is recorded in Parkin's book *Out of the Smoke*, which is one of the great stories of war at sea.

I met Parkin at Bandoeng, serenely sketching in water colours in a large, mixed, multiracial camp which when we were first marched into it struck Nichols and myself and our compact group of resolute men as singularly disorganized, if not utterly demoralized. From the moment of our first meeting Parkin became a close friend and ally. He too did many portraits and illustrations for our memorial book until he was sent away with a party of Australians to work on the infamous Burma–Siamese railway, an experience vividly described and illustrated in his book *Into the Smother*.

About half a dozen of his Bandoeng portraits and sketches survived the war because they were among those carried by Group-Captain Nicolettes, the most senior Royal Air Force officer in our camp, to Manchuria and returned to me afterwards.

Had I in my possession all the material produced by the arts and crafts faculty of our prison university, this book would have been rich indeed with impressive illustrations but alas! only a small portion of the work survived captivity. From the beginning of 1943 onwards as the special Japanese prison administration gained in power and confidence, the conditions of our imprisonment rapidly deteriorated. Our guards became more brutal, our rations steadily diminished, our prisons became more and more congested and our life increasingly uncertain. This melancholy and disturbing decline is to some extent recorded in a guarded prison diary I began to keep on December 14, 1942, and continued until November 26, 1943, a period of nearly a year.

It begins in Afrikaans as follows: "Yesterday was my birthday, the first in prison. In the morning I went to Church. In the afternoon a meeting of the trustees of the Memorial Book. Later in the day the rain came down heavily and there was lightning."

I began it in Afrikaans because I realized that keeping a diary, in however guarded a fashion, was a dangerous thing to do. I thought at first that the Japanese would not know what to make of Afrikaans, but I quickly abandoned the idea because I realized that not knowing would have an even worse effect on our captors than knowing, and would immediately give their suspicious imaginations full rein. My experience had already taught me to fear their imaginations more than their knowledge. I very soon, therefore, switched over into English and kept the diary on the whole confined to recording just enough of fact and statistics, with a slanted and obscure word or two here and there inserted to serve as a spur, I hoped, in years to come, to remembering the full reality of our life in prison.

This diary faithfully records the progressive decline in our dismal fortunes throughout 1943 and the circumstances in November which made me decide that it was no longer either safe to keep a diary or any records on my person.

Earlier in the year, already foreseeing such an end, I had asked Group-Captain Nicolettes to take some of the memorial book material with him when he was transferred from our camp with some Dutch generals to imprisonment at Harbin in Manchuria. He indeed carried the portraits of Donaldson and Cicurel among others in the pack on his emaciated back, out of our camp, and restored them to me some years after the war. They must be among the most widely travelled portraits in existence.

The others were gathered together with my diary, material for our memorial book, and such camp records as we valued, and on the evening of November 26, 1943, they were tied in bundles, wrapped in ground sheets and buried late at night in different places in our camp. As far as I know only my diary, a small number of illustrations and some copies of *Mark Time* survived their interment in the dank soil of our camp. The bulk and by far the most precious part of what we had buried mysteriously vanished, even some material which I took the precaution of burying underneath the carcass of a pig which had died that evening. After capitulation, although I myself set a whole company of Japanese prisoners-of-war digging up the soil of our old camp from end to end, neither the skeleton of the pig nor what we had buried underneath it nor, for that matter, anything else buried anywhere in the camp, could be found.

This to me is a confirmation, slight as it is, of the peril in which we had daily lived, and which can still shake my memory. It shows how much more closely we were watched and informed upon and how, among the mixed population of our camp, we were interpenetrated with spies, to an extent that even my own questioning self, constantly on guard, never suspected. I say this because the pit in which we buried the pig, and underneath the pig our valuable consignment of camp documents, also contained a canvas bag full of precious stones which the Chinese merchant whom I mention in the story had confided to me for safe burial. Someone, I am certain, must have informed the Japanese of this fact and so provoked them into looting the grave in secret themselves. If their greed had not conquered their sense of duty, some of us might have been punished for this, surely with death.

On November 25, 1943, already I had noted: "Three more people back from Tjimahi [a hospital camp nearby]. They say food situation even in hospital is very bad. They seem to be afraid of a move. Like us they feel their time is up. Mad Harry had a parade for officers which he celebrated by killing cats in their presence. He would throw them high up into the air again and again until they were dead. Don and I had a late night session with our pigs" [my code for saying that we had been listening in on our secret radio to the news and in particular to an account, I seem to remember clearly, of the American landing in the Gilbert Islands].

The "Mad Harry" mentioned was our troops' nickname for one of the worst of our Korean guards. I had recorded this incident because in the past, whenever something of importance was about to happen to us, the tension it produced in our guards would seek relief in injury to such innocent animals that might have strayed into the camp and escaped our own daily pot or, if animals were not available, in wrecking such furniture as we had in the camp. Both animals and furniture, I had learnt, were proxies in their imaginations for the prisoners they guarded.

For instance, some weeks before, one of the worst "blitzes" on us had been preceded by this sort of dress rehearsal in which our proxies had been some rats caught by our Korean guards. They had amused themselves torturing the rats, among other ways, by blowing them up with bicycle pumps from behind until they were swollen almost like toy balloons. Laughingly, they would watch the rats stagger painfully around until the release of air brought them relief and enabled them to try and escape, when they would be recaptured, the process repeated and so on again and again until they died. Seeing this, I had known that something evil was in store for us as well.

Accordingly Mad Harry's behaviour and the news

brought in from Tjimahi must have decided me that the end of our "golden age" had come, because my last entry on November 26 begins: "This is my last entry because I can no longer afford to ignore the signs. I believe that we may be moved at any moment to Batavia and from Batavia, Heaven knows where. A definite phase of our lives as p.o.w.'s has come to an end. I wish this could have been a franker document. I do not think anyone could picture from it how humiliating our treatment has been, how in a land of plenty, had it not been for our own efforts, we would long since all have been dead of malnutrition. If our own side had been beaten in this war, I do not think we would have lived. We are lucky to be alive. We have had no chivalrous consideration ever from our captors but—something of this *but* may be in this diary—I do not know."

There follows a farewell message to my wife and family, and a request to them not to forget that we had fought a good war in a good cause and the remark that "our imprisonment has taught us all the more how good our cause is."

I go on then to say that a typical Javanese prisoner-of-war evening is gathering. I observe that in the officers' lines one of the most dreaded of the Japanese warrant officers, Gunzo Hoshino, to whom I gave the nickname of "Star of the Field," and a couple of his Eurasian informers were conducting a search of the Dutch quarters.

I end the diary: "It is raining very hard—the thunder

clouds are sitting on the top of Tankgoeboehan-praauw [the mountain called 'ship upside-down' mentioned in the story]. My address is 13, Cadogan Street, London S.W.3. Will anybody who might find this diary please return it to Ingaret Giffard there."

By some miracle, the mildewed little book was recovered by an officer of the Indonesian Nationalist Forces who knew me and returned it to me, together with some of the drawings I have described.

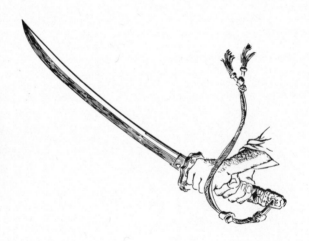